GREAT EVENTS
IN THE LIFE OF
DWIGHT D. EISENHOWER

5 Becomes assistant chief of staff to
General Douglas MacArthur, 1933

6 Appointed head of War Plans Division
of the War Department, 1942

8 Assumes presidency of
Columbia University, 1948

7 Becomes Supreme Commander of
Allied forces in Europe, 1943

THE STORY OF
Dwight D. Eisenhower

"The real job is just beginning"

THE STORY OF
Dwight D. Eisenhower

By ARTHUR J. BECKHARD

Illustrated by CHARLES GEER

ENID LAMONTE MEADOWCROFT
Supervising Editor

PUBLISHERS Grosset & Dunlap NEW YORK

PRINTED IN THE UNITED STATES OF AMERICA

LIBRARY OF CONGRESS CATALOG CARD NO. 57–5036

The Story of Dwight D. Eisenhower

Contents

[*v*]

Illustrations

THE STORY OF
Dwight D. Eisenhower

"Dwight, get up!" ordered Arthur

CHAPTER ONE
The Family

DWIGHT felt someone shake him and opened one eye just a slit. His oldest brother, fourteen, had him by the shoulder.

"Wake up! Wake up!" Arthur said and gave him another shake.

Dwight closed his eye quickly, pretending to be fast asleep.

"I would just as soon try to wake a log," muttered Arthur. "I never saw a ten-year-old boy who could sleep the way he does." He got off the bed and padded across the room. "Edgar! For the love of Mike, help me get Dwight out of bed," he said in a loud stage whisper. "It's five o'clock."

[3]

"Oh, go duck your head!" twelve-year-old Edgar told him. "I've got fifteen minutes more to sleep."

"A lot of help you are! If anything is done around here, looks like I have to do it myself," said Arthur in disgust. "But if Father wakes up and finds the fire isn't started, he'll whale us all."

Dwight, peeking at his brothers through his lashes, grinned to himself. Arthur was acting important again and trying to keep his younger brothers in line. He'd been doing it ever since Father had told them there was to be a new Eisenhower baby very soon and they would all have to give Mother more help with chores about the house.

Half the time, Dwight wanted to punch Arthur for this—and did. The other half, he had to laugh at him. Arthur could be pretty funny. Dwight's other brothers felt much the same way. That's why there were more than the usual number of noisy, good-natured skirmishes between the Eisenhower boys in the white frame house on South Fourth Street in Abilene, Kansas.

Dwight heard a padding of feet back across the floor and felt the bedcovers being tugged off him. He might have known Arthur would not give up so easily.

"Dwight, get up!" ordered Arthur. "It's your turn to chop the kindling for the fire."

In answer, Dwight snored loudly.

Just then, there was a loud wail from across the hall. Arthur left Dwight and dashed to the room where eight-year-old Roy slept with the baby.

"Roy, what's the matter with Earl?" he asked.

Dwight knew that one of the boys must have clapped a hand over the baby's mouth, for the wails were muffled now.

"Nothing's the matter with Earl," declared Roy. "He's a pretty smart kid, that's all. He always sits there on the register where the warm air comes up from the kitchen until I wake up to dress him. Well, he was just yelling to let me know there isn't any heat this morning."

"Pretty smart for a two-year-old," agreed Arthur. "Dwight was supposed to start the fire, and he just won't get up."

"I'll fix him," Roy said. "You dress Earl."

"Whatever you do, don't wake Father," Arthur cautioned him.

"I won't," Roy promised. "Something went wrong at the plant last night. I heard Mr. Hoffman come to get Father to go over and fix it."

David Eisenhower, the boys' father, had been mechanic-engineer at the Belle Springs Creamery since the family had moved to Abilene from Denison, Texas, where Dwight had been born.

"I guess Father must have worked 'most all night," Roy added.

"Then you had better not wake him or the fur will fly," warned Arthur. "And hurry up. I hate it, but I have to milk Betsy, clean out her stall, and let her out in the barnlot. Then I have to eat breakfast and be at school by eight-thirty. I can't wait around all day for you to get Little Ike out of bed."

Although their mother did not like the boys to use nicknames, Edgar was known as Big Ike and Dwight as Little Ike.

At that moment, Little Ike heard Roy going softly downstairs. Dwight was sure that Roy was planning to play some trick or other on him. He rolled onto his back, clasped his hands behind his head, and waited.

But Big Ike noticed Little Ike was awake

and came over to talk him into getting up.

"You're such a sleepyhead in the morning, suppose we swap jobs?" suggested Edgar.

Dwight shook his head. He did not like feeding the chickens and gathering eggs any better than Edgar did.

"All right, I'll give you my baseball glove if you will swap," Big Ike told him.

"No," said Little Ike. "No, I won't take it unless you give me your shin guards, too." He grinned impishly up at Big Ike.

"For that I'll give you this instead." And Edgar pushed a fist under Dwight's nose.

The next moment, Roy, sloshing water out of a big dipper, walked into the room. Arthur came too, carrying Earl. Roy's chubby face wore a broad grin. Tall, lean Arthur was struggling to look solemn. But the two were full of silent chuckles in anticipation of splashing cold water on the late sleeper. On seeing Dwight talking with Edgar, they stopped and stared.

Looking up at them, Dwight said, "Gee, thanks, Roy. How did you know I was thirsty?" He held out his hand for the dipper.

"Why, you—you—big faker!" sputtered Roy. "You were awake the whole time."

Arthur set Earl on the floor. Then, without a word, he and Roy and Edgar moved in toward Dwight.

"Hey, wait a minute!" cried Dwight, sitting up quickly. "Let me say something before you—"

"You said enough," Arthur interrupted him grimly. And they continued to close in on him.

"Look," Dwight said, "Edgar hates feeding the chickens. Arthur hates milking Betsy. And I hate getting up, so why can't we swap and—"

"That will do!" came their father's commanding voice from the doorway.

In sudden silence, the boys turned to face the quiet, dignified man.

"Since when has anyone been allowed to use the word *hate* in this house?" Mr. Eisenhower asked sternly.

At once the boys were ashamed. The Eisenhower family belonged to a religious group called the River Brethren. And one of their great beliefs was that people should not hate anyone or anything except evil itself. They believed that people should be kind and thoughtful of one another and live together in peace.

Mr. Eisenhower picked Earl up off the floor. "Now, what's all this talk of hating?" he asked.

"Well, I asked Dwight if he would swap jobs with me, because I—" Edgar stopped short before he said the word *hate*.

"Because you would rather do something else," his father finished for him. "You know your mother and I don't care how you boys work things out so long as the work gets done. But I *would* like Dwight to do the cooking this week. He's better at it than any of you." Mr. Eisenhower's dark eyes twinkled as he looked down at Dwight, who had begun to dress hastily. "I'll raise your allowance by five cents a week."

"Thank you, sir," Dwight said happily.

"But, Father," protested Edgar, "that sounds like a bribe."

Mr. Eisenhower looked very fierce for a moment, then his mouth widened in a smile. "If Dwight does the cooking he has to get up early and, of course, that means that you will all have to get up earlier to get him up in time to cook. So I'm going to raise all allowances by five cents."

"Hooray!" they all shouted. "Thanks, Father!"

[*9*]

"David Eisenhower! Boys! Come down this minute!" It was their mother's voice from the foot of the stairs.

Arthur, Edgar, Dwight, and Roy went tearing down the steps. Mr. Eisenhower followed, carrying Earl.

In the kitchen, the boys clustered around their mother, wanting to know if they had waked her with their noise.

"Of course you did," she told them. "While you were romping upstairs I got the fire started." At Dwight's crestfallen face, she softened her words by adding, "I began to feel hungry, so I was going to get up anyway."

Ida Eisenhower was a little woman, gay and warm. But she had a fiery spirit. Now, when she said, "Hurry up, boys, and get the chores done so we can have breakfast," they scattered to their various jobs without any nonsense.

Dwight got out the eggs and bacon and began fixing the meal. Edgar took care of the cow. Arthur looked after the chickens. Roy cared for the horse. Mr. Eisenhower left to get ready to go to work at the creamery.

With the baby hanging to her skirts, Mrs.

Eisenhower went about humming and cleaning up the house. Every once in a while she looked in on young Dwight D. to see how he was coming with his cooking. But, for the most part, she left him alone. A boy learned by doing. She believed that if her sons followed a few basic rules, whether in cooking or behavior, they could get along very well without much supervision.

When the boys came in from their chores, Dwight had breakfast on the table. The family sat down, and Mr. Eisenhower said grace. There was silence while everybody began eating flapjacks, eggs, bacon, and cornmeal mush.

Suddenly Roy spoke up. "Mother, I hope the new baby is a brother. Then we could have a first-class basketball team. We would have a substitute and everything."

"Don't be silly," said Arthur. "By the time even Earl here is old enough to play basketball, I'll be off somewheres."

"Learning to be a doctor perhaps," suggested Mrs. Eisenhower hopefully. She had always wanted one of the boys to be a doctor.

But Arthur shook his head. "No, there's

no real money in doctoring," he said.

"Since when are you so interested in money?" asked his father.

"It's not the money so much, I guess," re-

plied Arthur. "It's just that I'm tired of being snooted by the Northsiders. You ought to see, every time we go over there to sell vegetables they all act so stuck up."

The Eisenhowers lived on the South Side of the railway tracks which ran through Abilene. There the poorer people of the town lived. Across the tracks on the North Side

were the fine homes of the more wealthy townsmen.

"I want to be a big, successful business-man," chimed in Edgar. "Then I'd go live in a big house across the tracks and show those Northsiders a thing or two."

"But all sorts of people live on the North Side, besides businessmen," said Mrs. Eisenhower. "Doctors, lawyers, teachers—lots of different people. I used to like to study law. Maybe you'll be a lawyer, Edgar."

All of a sudden Roy gave a deep sigh that made everyone turn toward him. "If only brother Paul hadn't died," he said, "maybe someday we could have had an all-Eisenhower baseball team."

"Roy Eisenhower! What a thing to say!" cried Arthur.

"Now, Arthur, there is no reason why we shouldn't talk of Paul because he is no longer here with us," Mrs. Eisenhower told him quietly. "In our hearts he is with us." Then she smiled across at Dwight. "You had better bring us some more pancakes. I see the plate is empty."

While Dwight was busy at the stove, Mr. Eisenhower went over the day's program for the boys. "Arthur, I'd like you to take Beauty to Mr. Musser's to be shod this afternoon after school. Edgar and Dwight, you will have to sell the vegetables from the handcart instead of the wagon. And Roy, you can bring my lunch down to the plant."

"All of us ought to be through working in time to play Teddy Roosevelt and His Rough Riders," said Dwight, returning to the table with a plate stacked high with pancakes.

"Sure we will!" shouted the others.

"Straight up San Juan Hill, men! Charge!" Roy shouted at the top of his lungs and speared a flapjack.

"That war game with all of you whooping and waving sticks at each other!" said Mrs. Eisenhower. "Oh dear. Can't you play a less bloodthirsty game?"

"Aw, Mother, we don't hurt anybody. And it's such a lot of fun," said Dwight.

"You know, when I was at Lane University, we played a game that was fun," said Mr. Eisenhower. "We would take a pole with a piece of cloth at the top for a flag, and stick it in the ground. Then we would form two teams. One team linked arms and stood in a ring around the pole. Then the other team tried to break the ring to capture the flag. We would struggle hot and heavy there—one team trying to get the flag; the other team trying to keep them from getting it. We had the time of our lives."

"Sounds like a good game," Arthur said.

"But we haven't enough for two teams," said Roy. "Of course, if the new baby is a brother, there will be six of us."

"Well," warned Mr. Eisenhower with mock seriousness, getting up from the table, "all I can say is, I hope you boys have a little sister this time. Because, if you don't, I am going to pack my suitcase and go away."

"When all the boys grow up and get married," said Mrs. Eisenhower, laughing, "the house will be overflowing with girls." Glancing at Arthur, she said, "You had best be off. Remember, you have to go halfway across town to school now."

"Yes, Mother," Arthur said. Rising from the table, he went dashing upstairs for his books.

"Well, I guess I had better start making beds," said Roy. And he followed Arthur.

Since Dwight and Edgar had only to go across the street to the Lincoln school, they still had plenty of time. They began cleaning off the table.

When Mr. Eisenhower left for the creamery a few minutes later, the house was buzzing with activity. But that was not unusual for the Eisenhowers. They were one of the busiest, happiest families in Abilene.

CHAPTER TWO

Fresh Vegetables

THAT AFTERNOON Dwight and Edgar
were loading the red cart with vegetables to
sell when Grandfather Eisenhower came into
the yard. He carried Earl on one arm. Roy
was tugging at his other arm and pleading,
"Grandfather, can't we go hunt for hickory
nuts? It's not far."

"I know it's not far to the edge of town,"
replied Grandfather. "But we'll go some
other time, Roy. Has Arthur taken the horse
to be shod?" he asked Edgar.

"Not yet, Grandfather," answered Edgar.

"He's out in the pasture catching Beauty
now," said Dwight.

Dwight and Edgar suddenly became very

[*18*]

busy finding a safe place for the basket of eggs among the sweet corn and late string beans. They hoped Grandfather would leave before Arthur appeared. It would save a great deal of explaining.

But Grandfather was interested to see how neatly they piled the vegetables in the cart, so he stood watching. And in a few minutes, Arthur came by, leading Beauty on a halter rope.

He tried to hurry past, but Grandfather caught a glimpse of his face and stopped him.

"Been fighting again, I see," said Grandfather.

Arthur's left eye was all puffy, and the skin was beginning to turn purple.

"Yes, sir," admitted Arthur. "But it was in a good cause," he added quickly.

"He did it to protect somebody," Edgar said.

"It was on account of me," Dwight said.

Grandfather's eyes were stern. The grave old man in his farmer's clothes had been a preacher to members of the River Brethren. He did not approve of the boys' fighting any more than their parents did. However, Grandfather would admit that it might be necessary at times to fight for what was right and good.

So now Dwight explained, "Karl Briney was making fun of me because I wear Mother's high-button shoes to school."

His grandfather's face softened. The boys' father did not earn a large salary. It was hard for their mother to keep five growing boys in clothing. So clothes were handed down from one to another. And since Dwight's feet were about the same size as his mother's, he often wore her shoes.

"I see," Grandfather Eisenhower said kindly. "And you fought this Karl Briney because he made fun of you, Dwight?"

"No, sir," answered Dwight. "I just told him I like these old shoes. I can drop-kick better in them than in any old square-toed shoes like his. With Mother's shoes, I can drop-kick better than anybody in Lincoln school," he ended proudly.

"He can, too," Edgar said. "But Briney went on laughing and pointing and making fun. It was after school was out, and Arthur came by. And Arthur saw what was going on, so he went in and took a poke at Briney."

"Briney's the biggest boy in school," Dwight said. "A lot bigger than Arthur."

"And Briney knocked Arthur down," continued Edgar. "But Arthur got up and came at Briney again. Then Briney knocked him down again. Then I went and punched Briney."

"Whoop-whoop-whoop!" cried Dwight, jumping up and down, slugging rights and lefts. "Edgar punched him good. Briney's nose was bloody, and he fell down. But we had to pick Arthur up. He could hardly stand, and his eye was all swelled up. And now

[*21*]

Father is going to be awfully mad at him."

"I don't think your father will be very angry," Grandfather Eisenhower said.

"Well, he doesn't like us to get licked," Dwight pointed out. "And Arthur was licked before Edgar pitched in."

Their grandfather smiled. "Perhaps it taught Briney a lesson at any rate," he said. "Maybe after this, he will think twice before making fun of any of the Eisenhower boys."

Dwight and Edgar started out of the yard with the cart. Grandfather and Earl and Roy walked behind them. Arthur followed with Beauty, and the little parade went down the dirt road.

When they reached the Musser home, where their aunt Amanda and uncle Chris lived, Grandfather stopped. "I have a message from your mother for your aunt Amanda," he told them. "Come, Roy, I'm taking you and Earl with me."

The other boys went on. Arthur turned in at the blacksmith shop with Beauty. Dwight and Edgar continued across the railroad tracks to the North Side of town.

They trundled the cart down the wide, pleasant streets and around to the back doors of the big houses. A knock on the kitchen door usually brought the lady of the house.

"No vegetables today," she might say.

Or, "I think the corn is a little too old." She would pull down the husks to puncture a few kernels with her thumbnail to prove she was right, then she would add, "No. No, the corn is not tender enough."

It was a discouraging business altogether, this selling vegetables. As a result, Edgar used to grumble most of the time.

"They," Edgar would say, meaning the Northsiders, "think they can treat us any way they like." And he would get quite angry. Dwight, on the other hand, did not seem to mind.

"Maybe we'll have better luck at the next place," was what he usually said.

"You are such a kid, you don't even know when you are being snubbed," Edgar always told him.

Today they pulled the cart along the streets and around to the kitchen doors on their regular route. At the very first house, they sold a dozen eggs.

"Yes, ma'am, strictly fresh, just gathered this morning," Dwight had said in answer to

[23]

"Yes, ma'am, strictly fresh," Dwight said

the lady's question as to their freshness.

Then, at the next house, the woman picked over all the garden stuff without buying anything.

And so it went with here and there a sale, until the boys were down to the last of the string beans. It was growing dark, and the chill of a September evening was setting in.

"Let's go home," Edgar suggested. "We'll be late for supper."

"How about trying one more place," Dwight said, "then we'll go." He never liked to give up on anything.

At last they found a house that they thought looked promising and went around to the back.

A woman opened the door. "Now, what do you boys want?" she demanded crossly, peering at them in the yellow light of the kerosene lamp. "I'm busy cooking supper. No, I don't want any beans," she said almost before Dwight could finish telling her what he had to sell. She started to close the door, then hesitated. "Let me see them."

Dwight held out the peck measure. "They are about the last we'll have from our garden this season," Dwight told her.

She took a handful of the beans and began snapping them. "A little too old. They are tough and stringy." She looked hard at the boys. "You are the Eisenhower boys, aren't you?" she said.

"Yes, ma'am," they replied.

"Then as soon as you have ripe apples in your orchard, you might bring some around," she said. With that she went inside and closed the door.

"Tough and stringy, my foot!" cried Edgar. "I could have thrown them at her for being so mean."

"You know something?" Dwight said. "When I grow up I'm never going to act mean to anybody."

When they got home, Dr. Nelson was just climbing into his old buggy, and Grandfather was looking very happy as he handed the doctor his satchel.

"Everything is all right. Your mother is fine. And we've got company," their grandfather called to the boys.

"The new baby!" exclaimed Edgar.

"I'll drop by tomorrow," Dr. Nelson said to Grandfather Eisenhower, as he drove off.

Arthur came trotting home on Beauty just

then. He halted in the middle of the road when he saw the doctor's buggy.

The boys' aunt Amanda came out on the side porch. "Arthur!" she called. "Go fetch your father. Tell him it's another boy."

Without a word, Arthur wheeled Beauty and set out at a gallop for the creamery.

"Dwight! Edgar! You boys will have to get supper," Aunt Amanda said. "I have my hands full with your new brother."

CHAPTER THREE

"I Guess We Deserved It"

THE new baby was named Milton. And he made more work for his five brothers at first, because their mother had to give much of her attention to him. The boys pitched in and helped with the cooking, washing, and house cleaning. They did some grumbling among themselves about the extra chores, but they never really complained. They were happy about having another brother.

When Dwight was not in school, his special job was looking after two-year-old Earl. Time would come for Earl's afternoon nap, and Dwight would put his brother in the baby carriage. Then, taking one of his school books, Dwight would lie down, grab the axle of the carriage with his toes, and rock Earl back and forth. That way he could study his lesson and put Earl to sleep at the same time. Dwight was quite pleased with himself for being able to do two things at once.

With the coming of spring Dwight and Edgar were put to transplanting their mother's tomatoes, cabbage, lettuce, and other plants in the garden. They made a good team: one boy dropping the plants in the holes, and the other filling in and packing the earth around them.

Later, during vacation, all the boys except Roy had odd jobs around the creamery where their father worked. Arthur was old enough to have a regular job, and he began saving money.

"I have to think of the future," Arthur said, very solemn and grown up. "I'll be going out into the world to make my own way before long."

Arthur was always talking to his brothers about going out into the world. He felt he would have a better chance somewhere else than in Abilene.

"I want to get into some business and work my way up," Arthur insisted. "I would never be able to do that here in my home town."

Dwight and Edgar decided that Arthur was very smart to think things out for himself. But they were having too much fun practicing with a football on the school athletic field and playing One Old Cat in the yard with the other boys to think much about ever leaving home. They had a fine time right there in Abilene. The two of them were nearly always running into an exciting adventure.

That spring there was a flood in Abilene. The town lay between Mud Creek and Smoky Hill River. Whenever there was an unusually heavy rain, the creek and the river overflowed their banks and flooded part of the land. Some of the streets became deep, muddy streams.

It was about noon one day when Dwight and Edgar were on their way to the creamery carrying a lunch to their father. They stopped on the railroad embankment to watch the tumbling water.

Suddenly Dwight cried, "Look!" and pointed to an old rowboat which had floated down the stream and lodged against the embankment. "Let's take a ride," he suggested.

He set down his father's lunchbox and scrambled down the embankment with Edgar close behind him.

"It's a leaky old tub," he remarked when they had reached the boat. "There's lots of water in it."

"And there aren't any oars, either," Edgar said. "Wonder who owns it."

Dwight shrugged his shoulders. "Whoever

he is, he isn't around," he said with a wide grin.

He stepped into the boat, and the water gurgled into his shoes. Edgar shoved the craft away from the bank, jumping into it as it moved off. A moment later the boys were drifting down the muddy stream.

All at once Dwight leaned over the side of the boat and made a grab for a board.

"Watch out," Edgar cried. "You'll upset us!"

"No, I won't." Dwight hauled in the board. "Look, we can use this for a paddle. Say, what's that man over there yelling at us for?"

He motioned to a man who stood at one edge of the flooded area. The man's voice reached them across the swirling water.

"Want to make some money, you two?"

he called. "I'll pay you twenty-five cents if you'll row me over to the other side."

"Twenty-five cents!" Edgar exclaimed joyfully. He grabbed the board from his brother and began to paddle with all his might.

Twenty-five cents seemed like a lot of money to the young Eisenhower boys. And it was fun to play ferryman, even though it was not easy to steer and to paddle the heavy old rowboat with a single oar. Especially when that oar was nothing but an old board.

They were able at last to land their passenger safely just where he wanted to go. When he paid them, Edgar put the quarter in his pocket for safekeeping.

"This sure is an easy way to earn money," Dwight said. "Let's look around for some more customers."

Edgar thought this was a good idea. By this time, Dwight had rescued another board, and they paddled downstream, each keeping an eye out for someone else who might like to get across.

Pretty soon they saw three of their friends on the bank. Pulling into shore, they took them aboard. Then they went on again. Dwight had never been happier. He began to sing at the top of his lungs, "Mine eyes have seen the glory of the coming of the Lord," and the others joined in.

They were floating down a large ditch now, and having such a good time that they paid no attention to two big boys who stood on the bank just ahead of them. As the boat passed, one of the older boys grabbed it by the bow, and both of them jumped in.

It was already low in the water. Now it began to sink rapidly. A moment later all seven boys were floundering around in the stream. Fortunately it was not very deep. Soaking wet and covered with mud, they clambered up on the bank.

Mr. Volkman, one of the Eisenhowers' neighbors, was passing by. He stopped to watch them and recognized two of them at once.

"Edgar Eisenhower!" he said sternly as the boys reached the sidewalk which ran along the bank. "And you, Dwight! Your mother's been looking everywhere for you. If you know what's good for you, you'll get home right away."

Dwight wiped some mud from his eyes. "What's she want, Mr. Volkman?" he asked.

But before Mr. Volkman could answer, Edgar moaned, "Father's lunch! We forgot to take it to him. Mother will be awful mad."

He darted down the street toward home. Dwight followed, the water spurting from his shoes as he ran. When they neared the house, both boys slowed down.

"Do you think she'll whip us?" Dwight asked.

Edgar nodded. "Look," was all he said.

There on the steps stood their mother, holding two stout switches.

"Do you know what time it is?" she asked sternly. "It's past three o'clock, and your poor father hasn't had a bite to eat since breakfast. Get yourselves upstairs and take off those filthy, wet clothes."

She stepped aside to let them pass. Feeling very much ashamed, they went upstairs. Without another word, Mrs. Eisenhower followed them. When they were undressed she gave them each a whipping they remembered for a long, long time. Then she told them both to go to bed and stay there.

"Since your father had to do without his lunch, you can do without your suppers," she said, gathering up the wet clothes. And she left the room, closing the door behind her.

Dwight buried his face in his pillow, determined not to cry.

"That's the *worst* whipping I ever had," Edgar remarked softly.

"Me, too," Dwight said in a muffled voice. "But I guess we deserved it." He rubbed his legs, which still smarted. "What happened to the quarter?"

"Don't know," Edgar replied sadly. "I felt for it in my pocket as we came upstairs, and it wasn't there. It must have fallen out when we were dumped into the water." He sighed. "Twenty-five cents is a lot to lose."

Dwight turned over in bed. "Yep, but I guess we deserved that, too," he said.

And Edgar agreed.

CHAPTER FOUR

The Big Fight

DWIGHT felt lost the year Edgar began going to Garfield High School. They had been in school together, played on the same teams, and worked together. Now, there were many days that he and Edgar did not see each other from breakfast until supper. Then, when they did get together, Edgar acted very high and mighty toward his younger brother.

Of course, Edgar had reason to strut a bit. He had become a school hero almost overnight. Each year, the boys at Garfield chose one boy to represent the South Side students and another boy to represent the North Side. The two boys then fought each other for the championship of the school. This year Edgar was chosen to be the South Side boy, and Karl Briney, the North Side. With his second punch, Edgar had knocked out Karl, and had become champion of Garfield High.

It was a great victory not only for Edgar, but also for the Southsiders. In fact, it was a sort of victory for better feelings all around.

After the fight, Karl and Edgar became good friends. And Edgar was as popular with the students north of the tracks as he was with those south of the tracks.

From that success, Edgar had gone on to another. He had made the first squad on the

[39]

football team and was fast growing into the best halfback the school ever had.

Edgar's free time was spent in football practice. He no longer had time to play with boys of Dwight's age. And this superior attitude used to make Dwight's quick temper go off like a bunch of firecrackers. The time came when Edgar could hardly say or do anything without Dwight taking offense and trying to start a fight.

Although Edgar won every tussle, Dwight never gave up. He wanted to lick Edgar just once. That would prove to Edgar that he could be licked, and Dwight would be satisfied.

The loss of Edgar's companionship at school and play was bad enough. But that fall, Edgar took a job helping Sheriff Brown make apple butter. The Browns' orchard was not far from the Eisenhower place. From the yard at home, Dwight could see the smoke rising from the fire under the big copper kettle set under the apple trees.

Watching the smoke and thinking about Edgar working over there without him made Dwight feel completely deserted. If only he and Edgar had still shared jobs, he might not have felt so alone and left out of things.

And to make it worse, Edgar usually came home from Sheriff Brown's all cock-a-hoop and full of exciting stories.

"You know what Mr. Brown told me to-day?" Edgar would begin right after Mr. Eisenhower had asked the blessing at the supper table. "He told me that Abilene used to be one of the toughest towns in the West. You wouldn't believe it, would you? Nothing ever happens here now. Well, you see the way it was, Abilene was the end of the Chisholm Trail. And the Texans used to drive their longhorn cattle up this trail to Abilene to load on the Union Pacific Railway. So . . ."

And Edgar would launch into a long story about the early days of the Old West, with cowboys shooting and gambling and causing all kinds of trouble. Sheriff Brown had lived during the days of the cattle drives, and he was chock full of yarns about cowboys, mustangs, and Texas longhorns.

Dwight would have given almost anything to be able to work with Edgar making apple butter for Sheriff Brown.

Instead, Dwight still had the vegetable

[*41*]

route. His new partner was Roy, who was a good helper. In a number of ways, he was even better than Edgar. For one thing, Roy never grumbled.

They would draw up their cart to the back porch of a house where the woman was very hard to please. She would strip the corn, punch the melons, and jab the peaches. Then she might toss it all back in the cart without buying anything. If Edgar had been along, he would have boiled over. But not Roy. His good nature never left him. His blue eyes danced, and his chubby face remained cheerful.

"No use getting mad at her," Roy would say to Dwight. "She has to find fault with everything. It's her nature. Probably when the clerks see her coming into a store, they run and hide to keep from waiting on her." And Roy would laugh about it.

Roy did not mind either, having to take Milton with them occasionally.

"I think Milton helps business," Roy insisted. Then he would laugh and make a big joke out of it.

Truth was, Dwight had to admit that the baby did help. Milton with his hazel eyes and brown curls made a pretty picture sitting among the carrots and tomatoes and garden greens. He attracted people to the vegetable cart who otherwise would never have given it a second glance. Once they stopped to admire the baby, people often bought a head of lettuce, a bunch of onions, or a basket of peaches.

Then one day when all the boys were out in the yard with a group of their friends, Roy thought of playing the ring game with Milton. With Milton taking the place of the flag, Arthur, Edgar, Dwight, Earl, and Roy held hands with their backs to the baby, and defied their friends to break through and touch him. This changed looking-after-Milton from an often tiring chore into an exciting game.

Although Roy was a good partner in work and they had a lot of fun together, Dwight missed Edgar. For one thing, he could not talk to Roy the way he could to Edgar. And, for another, they did not enjoy doing things together the way he and Edgar did. Dwight always thought of Roy, Earl, and Milton as "the little ones." Arthur, Edgar, and himself were "the big ones." To Dwight, Roy was still just a little kid.

About the time Dwight was feeling very

alone and neglected, he became acquainted with "Swede" Hazlett and "Six" MacDonell.

"To nickname a boy Swede is bad enough," Dwight's mother said. "But why do you call that nice MacDonell boy Six?"

"You remember when that art exhibit came to town a few weeks ago?" Dwight asked.

Mrs. Eisenhower nodded.

"Well, all of us in school went to see it," Dwight went on. "This exhibit was reproductions of the world's great paintings. And there was a man who explained them to us. When he came to the picture of a sad-looking woman, he kept calling it the Sixteen MacDonell. Anyway, that's what it sounded like."

"Sixteen MacDonell?" His mother was puzzled.

"Yes, Mother. We all thought the man said, 'Sixteen MacDonell.' So right away, all the boys began calling John MacDonell, *Sixteen MacDonell*. You see?" Dwight laughed. "Of course, the teacher told us later that it was The Sistine Madonna, painted by Raphael for the Church of San Sisto. It's in the Royal Gallery at Dresden now."

"I still don't see why you boys have to use nicknames," Dwight's mother said tartly.

"All of you have perfectly good first names."

"Six" was two years younger than Dwight, but he was an outstanding baseball player. Because of this, Dwight overlooked the difference in ages.

Six introduced Dwight to Joe Howe, the editor of the *Dickinson County News*. Mr. Howe had brought together a group of boys, called the Knights of Honor. They had their clubhouse in the basement of the newspaper office and met there off and on during the month to play games or plan projects. They went fishing and hiking, played baseball, and did many things together.

Dwight got along well with all the boys and enjoyed being with them. It was fine to have friends, he found. All the same, he waited anxiously for the time to come when he would enter Garfield High School. He dreamed of being on the football team and becoming a greater star than Edgar.

At last the longed-for September came. Dwight was enrolled in the freshman class at the high school. But he had built his hopes very high, only to find that some of the things he had planned did not turn out as he had expected.

He and Edgar were now in the same school,

it was true, but they were in different classes.
Edgar played on different teams. He was a
sophomore, and sophomores were inclined
to feel somewhat above mere freshmen.

Upon trying out for the football team,
Dwight had another disappointment. Mr.
Hoffman, the coach, put him in the line at
tackle.

"Please give me a chance at end or back,"
Dwight pleaded.

Mr. Hoffman studied the slender, sandy-
haired youngster. The blue eyes were looking
directly at him. The coach decided that anything but the blunt truth would be insult-
ing to such a boy.

"Dwight," Mr. Hoffman told him, "in the
first place, you aren't fast enough. And, in
the second place, you are too green. You can't
begin to think of competing with players
like your brother Edgar yet."

Dwight swallowed his hurt pride. "All
right then, Mr. Hoffman," he said, "I'll play
tackle."

So he played tackle in all the practice scrim-
mages. But his hope of becoming a football
star was crushed. For all his practicing, he
was just not a good player.

Then the time arrived for the boys to be chosen to fight for the championship of the school. Dwight never dreamed he would be considered. But to his surprise, the South-siders elected him. Dwight's spirits rose.

"Now maybe I'll be school champion just like Edgar," he thought.

He was unpleasantly surprised when the Northsiders elected a boy named Wes Merry-field. Wes weighed about twenty pounds more than Dwight and had longer arms. No one would have blamed Dwight if he had backed out of the contest. But Dwight made up his mind to fight. He would not think of letting his South Side friends down.

At five o'clock on the day of the match, a large crowd gathered in the vacant lot across the street from City Hall. Some of the boys formed a ring. Wes and Dwight went to their corners inside the ring.

All was quiet for a moment. Then the voice of the teen-age referee announced, "In that corner, wearing the blue jeans and no shirt, Dwight David Eisenhower, represent-ing the South Side."

A few of the students clapped. There were many who "booed."

[47]

"And in that corner," went on the young referee, "wearing the white trunks and long underwear, Wes Merryfield, representing—"

His voice was drowned out by the cheers of the North Side boys and girls.

The Southsiders began to size up the two boys. Dwight seemed to grow smaller and thinner, the more they compared him with the big, husky Wes. Dwight surely could not win against that brawny slugger. But they knew that Dwight would do his best, so they cheered loudly to encourage him.

"Quiet! Quiet!" yelled the referee. "The championship bout of Garfield High School is about to begin. Will the two champions step into the center of the ring?"

Dwight and Wes walked out from their corners.

"You know the rules," the referee told them. "No kicking, no wrestling, no blows below the belt."

The boys nodded.

"No rounds, no time out," went on the referee. "This is a fight to the finish. Is that understood?"

The boys nodded again.

"Now, shake hands," said the referee. "Go

[*48*]

to your corners and, when I whistle, come out fighting."

At the referee's whistle, Dwight charged out of his corner and tried to land a haymaker. He flung a series of lefts and rights at Merryfield, without noticing the blows he himself was receiving.

Merryfield's weight and his longer arms were standing him in good stead. He was landing blow after blow to Dwight's face and ribs. Dwight just kept boring in.

After five minutes of toe-to-toe slugging with neither boy taking a back step, it began to be seen that Dwight was losing the contest. The South Side rooters were ready to admit defeat. But Dwight fought on doggedly. Although Merryfield was landing more and more punches, Dwight plugged away.

The cheering, shouts, and jibes ceased. As the minutes dragged by, the crowd fell silent. In the growing dust, only the sound of fists hitting flesh or bone broke the stillness. The clock in the City Hall tower struck six. An hour had passed.

Some of the boys began to be uneasy. Six o'clock was suppertime. If they were late getting home, they would be in trouble. But they stayed on, fascinated by the desperate struggle between the pair. Then, little by little, the crowd became aware that the situa-ion in the ring had changed. All the sting had gone out of Wes Merryfield's punches while Dwight was boring in with greater con-fidence.

Dwight, too, sensed a change in Wes. His

opponent no longer seemed sure of himself. There was a puzzled look on his face. In spite of weariness, pain, and eyes almost swollen shut, Dwight redoubled his efforts.

A murmur ran through the crowd. They had seen enough. What had seemed a fine and brave fight was turning into something silly and stupid. What they had thought was great courage was becoming nothing but

senseless stubbornness. They began to leave.

The two boys were out on their feet. Their arms hung at their sides like lead weights. All they could do was bump, push, and shove each other.

Finally, Merryfield grunted and, using his last ounce of strength, pushed Dwight away from him and stepped back.

"I can't lick you, Dwight," he said thickly.

Weaving slightly from side to side to keep from falling, Dwight looked groggily at Wes. His lips were terribly cut and bruised, but he managed a grin. "I haven't licked you either, Wes," Dwight said. As the clock began to strike, he peered up at City Hall tower. "But I guess it took us two hours to find it out."

It was seven o'clock. They had been fighting since five.

Most of the onlookers had gone home. The few who remained rushed in to hold up the tottering fighters. Several took Wes off with them.

Six and Swede helped Dwight home. They took him up the back stairs, undressed him, bathed his bruises, and bound up his cuts. Then they put him to bed where he lay without moving.

After the boys had left, Mr. Eisenhower came up to the room.

"Do you know how much you've hurt your mother, fighting this way?" demanded his father. When there was no answer, Mr. Eisenhower leaned down. "Were you fighting for something you believed in?" he asked.

"No, sir," Dwight mumbled.

"Fighting for the sake of fighting is a sin," his father said sternly. Then his eyes suddenly twinkled, and his face melted into the Eisenhower grin. "Did you win?" he asked eagerly.

"No, sir," answered Dwight. "But I didn't lose, either."

Then he heard his father say kindly, "Good night," and the door closed softly. Dwight fell asleep.

CHAPTER FIVE

"Go, Team, Go!"

DWIGHT was not very happy over the Big Fight. He had longed to be the champion, the hero of the school as Edgar had been, and he had failed. It was a sad disappointment.

On the Saturday of the football game between the freshmen of Kansas University and Garfield High School, Dwight sat on the bench. He watched the game, aching to be out on the field.

The Garfield team was strong on defense. The Kansas freshmen were unable to get through the Garfield line. And every end run was stopped by the fine defensive play of Edgar at halfback and the other boys backing up the line.

When Garfield got possession of the ball, however, they could not gain an inch. The Kansas team simply "smeared" Edgar. Every time he was given the ball, he was smothered before he could take a step.

The first half of the game ended in a scoreless tie.

In the gym locker room, between the halves, Mr. Hoffman praised the boys. "Try harder to break Edgar loose," the coach told them. "If you can do that, you can beat Kansas."

His gaze traveled over the Garfield linemen: Six MacDonell and Swede at guard, Wes Merryfield at center, Bud Hoffman and Nick Carter at end, and Jameson and Moore at tackle. He nodded with satisfaction. "I think you can do it," he said.

Mr. Hoffman did not even glance in Dwight's direction.

The team went out on the field. Dwight took his place on the bench.

As the second half began, the Kansas kickoff was poor and Jameson at tackle caught the ball. At once the Kansas team piled up on him. When the boys rose from the pile-up, Kansas had recovered the ball, and Jameson lay where he had fallen. Garfield called for time out. Jameson was helped off the field by a couple of the players.

Dwight felt the coach's hand on his shoulder. "Go out there, boy," said the coach. "Don't be too eager. Don't try to be a hero. *Just help hold that line.*"

This was his chance, Dwight thought excitedly. He dashed onto the field.

"Who do you think you are, Eisenhower?" Pee Wee Barton, the quarterback, demanded furiously. "Go back and get your headguard!"

Sheepishly, Dwight ran back, picked up his headguard, and hurried to his position.

The Kansas quarterback directed the first play through Dwight. And through Dwight it went. The husky linemen tossed him out of the way as easily as blowing the fluffy top off a dandelion. The halfback went plunging through for ten yards and a first down.

The Kansas team tried the same play again, then again. They succeeded both times. Then, to Garfield's surprise, Kansas tried it for the fourth time.

The ball-carrier fought his way into the clear. Edgar dove for his knees and missed. There was only the Garfield fullback between the Kansas runner and the goal line. The full-back tried to stop him, but the Kansas player dodged away and sprinted across the line for a touchdown.

The Kansas freshman led Garfield High, five to nothing. Then point after touchdown was made. It was Kansas 6, Garfield 0.

Dwight was disgusted with himself. He had been given a chance to hold the line, and he had failed. He was a complete flop. He felt terrible.

Just then Pee Wee slapped him on the shoulder. "Cheer up, kid," he said. "You did your best. Now get back in there."

Dwight was amazed that the other players did not want to throw him out of the game. Then he looked toward the sidelines. There was Fatso Walpole warming up. Was the coach going to replace him with Fatso, the worst player on the team? Dwight gritted his teeth. He could not bear to have that happen.

But try as he would, Dwight could not improve his playing. Pee Wee was afraid that Dwight could not open up a path for the Garfield ball-carriers. So he sent the plays around the other side or tried end-runs, without success.

With time running out and Kansas in possession of the ball, Dwight suddenly had an idea. He whispered it quickly to Six and Swede. They nodded and took their positions in the line.

The ball was snapped, and again the Kansas quarterback came at Dwight. This time, as though he were afraid of getting hurt, Dwight scuttled out of the way. As the two-man interference swept by him, Dwight quickly jumped back into position, dumping the ball-carrier two yards behind the line of scrimmage.

The Kansas team evidently thought what had happened was an accident. So they tried the play again. This time Dwight nailed his man for a four-yard loss. Kansas tried the other side of the line on the next play, but the Garfield line held. Kansas lost possession of the ball on their own thirty-five-yard line.

On the first play, the Garfield tackles opened up a hole for the ball-carrier for a two-yard gain. Then Pee Wee sent the play

through Dwight's side. Dwight and Six opened up a hole for Edgar for a four-yard gain. A quarterback sneak added six yards for a first down.

Dwight, Six, and Wes with crunching body-blocks opened a hole for Edgar, and he charged through it.

Bud and Nick, the two fastest men on the team, closed in from their end positions. Edgar picked up his interference and kept on going. Seventeen yards!

"We want a touchdown! We want a touchdown! We want a touchdown!" chanted the crowd.

The Garfield team was afire now. It was working together like a powerful machine.

A hole opened in the line, and Edgar broke into the clear. With Dwight running interference, Edgar flashed down the sideline and crossed the goal line standing up.

Touchdown for Garfield! Kansas University led 6 to 5. Pee Wee added the extra point, and the two teams were tied.

The crowd roared. "Go, team, go!" they screamed. "Do it again! Do it again!" they yelled at Edgar.

Garfield kicked off. The Kansas team was grim. The Kansans could hear the jeering they would get back in Hutchinson if they returned to the University as losers to a bunch of high school kids. They drove and strained, but they could not get past the Garfield line.

Then, with only a minute and a half left to play, the Kansas quarterback called for a punt on last down.

The kicker tried to keep the ball away from Edgar, Garfield's speedy safety man. On the dead run, Edgar, however, managed to make a shoestring catch. Without breaking stride, he broke for the south sideline and headed for the distant Kansas goal.

The Garfield team quickly formed a wedge to run interference for him.

"Come on, Edgar!" the crowd yelled.

Kansas players were cut down all over the field. At last, only the fullback was left between Edgar and the goal line. Bud and Nick drove in from opposite sides and chopped him down with a tremendous high-low block. Edgar danced across the goal without a hand being laid on him.

A moment later, the signal came, ending the game.

The crowd surged out of the stands and onto the field. The Garfield team was swamped by boys and girls, all shouting and yelling joyfully.

"Snake dance!" someone shouted.

And they all began to chant, "We want Big Ike! We want Big Ike! Good old Ike!"

Dwight and several of the team hoisted Edgar to their shoulders. The twisting, turning parade started down the field. Dwight was completely happy. He did not want to change places with Edgar. He was satisfied just to play on the Garfield team. He knew now what real teamwork meant. Without it, Edgar would never have made the touchdown that won the game for Garfield.

Half an hour later, while both teams were sponging themselves off with hot water in the gym locker room, Mr. Hoffman came in with Joe Purdy, the director of athletics at Kansas University.

"Well, team," Mr. Purdy said to the Kansas freshmen, "you played fine football out there this afternoon. You don't have to be ashamed to go back home. You were beaten by a better team, that's all. A team with splendid team spirit. When a bunch of boys has the kind of spirit Garfield had this afternoon, it is practically unbeatable." He paused and looked around. "Where is young Eisenhower?" he asked.

Dwight looked at Edgar and motioned for him to step forward. Edgar shrugged and

shook his head. Then Dwight realized that
Mr. Purdy was looking at him.

"You want me, sir?" Dwight asked.

"I only wanted to tell you that good linemen are hard to find," said Mr. Purdy. "Most
of the good men want to play in the backfield
because it is showier. Judging by your play
today, I think you have a chance to be one
of the best tackles in the game, a year or two
from now. So stick to it."

Cheers and shouts broke out all over the
gym locker room. Karl Briney jumped up
from the bench on which he was sitting and
cried, "A cheer for Little Ike! Come on, everybody! Hip-hip-hip hooray!"

The others joined in.

Dwight stole a glance at Edgar, who appeared puzzled and hurt. Then he whispered
to Six, "How about a cheer for Big Ike, too?"

"Sure," replied Six. "A cheer for Big Ike,"
he shouted.

"Hip-hip-hip hooray! Hip-hip-hip hooray!
Big Ike!" cheered the team.

Dwight felt embarrassed about facing Edgar alone, so he dressed quickly and hurried
out of the school. He started for home at a
brisk walk. But he had hardly gone two
blocks when he heard, "Hey, wait for me!"

Turning around, he saw Edgar running toward him down the street. Edgar came up and, without saying a word, the two walked along together. They went about a block, then Dwight felt Edgar's arm drop across his shoulders.

"Nice going, Little Ike," Edgar said. "I been thinking that if we worked together and practiced in the yard, we could come up with some pretty good plays."

"Say, that would be great!" cried Dwight.

"As a matter of fact," Edgar went on, "I have an idea for using what you did this afternoon. Use it on the offense instead of the defense. Here's the way it works; see what you think of it."

All the rest of the way home, they discussed the idea of "mouse-trapping" over-eager defensive linemen. All the while they flew about doing their evening chores, they talked football. So they could go on talking football, they made a swap of jobs with Arthur and Roy, and washed and dried the supper dishes together.

"Football, football, football," said Roy, dumping the morning's kindling wood into the woodbox. "Why don't you talk about something else for a change?"

Dwight and Edgar paid not the least attention to Roy. Back on their old friendly relations with each other, they were thoroughly enjoying themselves.

When all the chores were done, the family gathered in the front room.

Mr. Eisenhower brought out the Bible. Opening it to a page which he had marked from the last reading, he handed the Bible to Dwight. "Suppose you begin," he said.

Dwight read almost a page before Roy caught him making a mistake. Dwight had mispronounced a word, so he had to let Roy have the privilege of reading. The Bible was passed from one to another, as the readers were caught in mistakes. The family played the game so often, even little Earl was able to catch a mistake once in a while.

A few minutes past eight, Mr. Eisenhower closed the Bible and put it away on the shelf. Going to the clock which hung on the wall, he wound it. That was the signal for bedtime.

Dwight and Edgar said good night to their parents and went upstairs together. Suddenly Dwight said, "You know, it's true."

"What's true?" asked Edgar, yawning.

"What it says in Ecclesiastes," replied Dwight. "What we were just reading tonight." Then he quoted, " 'Better is the end of a thing than its beginning; and the patient in spirit is better than the proud in spirit.' "

"What made you bring that up?"

"Oh, I was just thinking about the football game," answered Dwight. "The end sure was better than the beginning. And when I quit being—well, proud in spirit, trying to win all by myself, everything went a lot better."

CHAPTER SIX

Dwight and Edgar Make a Pact

ARTHUR, who always talked of going out into the world to make his own way, was at last leaving Abilene. He was going to Kansas City to hunt for a job.

Mrs. Eisenhower felt the family would make too big a show of themselves if they were all to see him off at the railroad station. So all of them, including Grandfather Eisenhower, Aunt Amanda and Uncle Chris Musser, had gathered on the side porch to bid Arthur good-by.

Dwight and Edgar were out in the yard by the porch, throwing a baseball back and forth. Since early spring, they were seldom seen without bat and ball. At Garfield High, they practically ran the baseball team.

"Aren't you two boys going to stop playing long enough to tell your brother good-by?" their mother called from the porch to Dwight and Edgar.

"Yes, Mother. Just as soon as Arthur comes down, we'll stop," answered Dwight.

"Well, you better stop right now," warned Roy, "because here he is."

Dwight tucked the ball into his side pocket, and he and Edgar ran up on the porch.

Arthur set his suitcase down and ran his fingers around inside his high, stiff collar. "Guess I'll have to get used to wearing one of these things every day now that I'm going to be a businessman," he said, grinning.

"That you will, son," agreed Mr. Eisenhower.

"You're sure you packed everything, Edgar?" asked his mother.

"Oh, yes, I have everything," he assured her.

Everyone fell silent, not knowing just what to say on this very important occasion. Arthur was the first of the Eisenhower boys to leave home.

Arthur himself broke the silence. "When

are you two going to quit eating and sleeping
baseball and start thinking about something
more important?" he demanded, glaring
fiercely at Dwight and Edgar. "You, especially, Edgar. Don't forget, you finish high

school in June." Then he gave them a big
grin to show them he was not really angry.
"I mean it. You boys ought to begin making
plans for the future."

"You needn't worry. I have a few ideas of
my own," said Edgar.

[69]

Dwight winked at Edgar. "Anyway, we thought we would wait and see how you did first," he said to Arthur.

"Never you mind, Dwight Eisenhower. Your brother is going to do all right," said Aunt Amanda.

"Well, I guess I had better get along," Arthur said. "I don't want to miss my train." He started around the family circle, shaking hands.

He hugged his mother, who told him sternly, "Now, you look after yourself."

"I will. I will, Mother." Picking up his suitcase, he went quickly down the porch steps.

They watched him walk away from the house, swinging his suitcase. At the corner, he turned and waved. They all waved back. A moment later, Arthur had turned the corner and disappeared.

"I don't know about the rest of you, but I have work to do," said Aunt Amanda.

She left with Uncle Chris. Mr. Eisenhower returned to the creamery. Grandfather went off somewhere with Earl and Milton. Some of Roy's friends came by, and they went to play marbles under one of the big maple trees. There were only Dwight, Edgar, and their mother left on the porch.

"I expect you are going over to the sandlot to play Saturday baseball as usual," she said.

"Yes, Mother," they told her.

"Well, just so you are home in time to do your chores," she said, smiling.

As the two Ikes went jogging toward the sandlot, Edgar said, "Arthur is right. I must begin right now to plan ahead, if I want to go to the University of Michigan to study law."

"Maybe you can get a scholarship at Kansas University," suggested Dwight. "You could study to be a lawyer there."

"No. I'd rather go away from Kansas," Edgar said. "I want to go some place where everything is new and different."

"I want to go to college, too," Dwight said.

"Then we had better start thinking," Edgar told him. "We have to figure out some way to get money for college."

The rest of that spring, the boys did some very serious thinking and planning. When summer came, they took jobs on a neighbor's farm. Each of them saved every penny he could. Yet, before the end of summer, Edgar realized that no matter how much he

[71]

worked and saved, he still would not have enough money for college.

"It's pretty discouraging," Edgar complained one evening as he and Dwight started for home across the field where they had been helping the farmer mow hay. "First I have to have money for college, and then law school. And then I have to be an apprentice in some law office. Sometimes it just seems hopeless."

"Unhuh," murmured Dwight. He was busy thinking. An idea had been growing in his mind for a long while. Maybe now was the time to tell it.

"I'm going to give you my savings," he blurted out. "Then you'll have enough."

"Oh, no! I won't take your money!" Edgar exclaimed. "You'll need it yourself."

"Look, I'll lend it to you," Dwight said. "And—"

"But how would I pay you back?" Edgar asked.

"Listen, will you?" Dwight said. "What I mean is, we'll pool our savings. You take them and go to college and—"

"Right," interrupted Edgar. "Then I can get a job at college, waiting on table or something, and pay my own expenses once I get there."

"I'll go on working in my spare time," continued Dwight, "and keep saving money. Then, next summer we can both work and I will be able to go to college on what we save. See?"

"Say!" cried Edgar. "That's a wonderful idea! I think we can do it, too."

"Of course, we can," Dwight assured him.

"Together, we can work it," said Edgar. He held out his hand. "Shake. It's a deal."

"It's a deal," Dwight repeated.

They shook hands solemnly.

The pact that Big Ike and Little Ike made with each other that day was a success. By the time Edgar was ready for college, the joint savings amounted to enough for him to enter the University of Michigan and pay expenses until he could get a spare-time job.

After Edgar left in September, Dwight worked at odd jobs in the creamery. When he was not in school or at work, though, he missed Edgar's companionship. It was very much like the time Edgar entered high school and left him behind in grammar school. Dwight was just as lonely. And often he was moody.

One morning he got up feeling particularly unhappy. And halfway to school, he suddenly decided to turn aside and take the path that led to the woods. He spent the whole day there.

The next day, he went to school as usual. Since he had no excuse to give the teacher for his absence the day before, he was sent to the principal.

"You simply played hookey," said the principal when Dwight explained what he had done.

"Yes, sir."

"Then I'm afraid you can't play in next Saturday's football game," the principal told him.

Dwight pleaded with the principal to let him play, but the principal refused. Dwight had played hookey and he had to take the consequences. After he had left the office, the more Dwight thought about it, the angrier he became. It was unfair not to let him play. He decided to go see his friend Mr. Howe, the editor of the *Dickinson County News*, who was on the school board.

"It isn't right just because I played hookey once to keep me out of the game Saturday," Dwight told Mr. Howe.

"Whether it is fair or unfair," said Mr.

"You simply played hookey," said the principal

Howe kindly, "I would not think of interfering with school discipline."

"Then you won't put in a good word for me, Mr. Howe?" asked Dwight.

Mr. Howe shook his head.

"But the whole team will suffer unless I can play," Dwight pointed out. "We've been practicing some of the plays for weeks and weeks."

"You should have thought of that before," Mr. Howe said drily. "Remember, in the Knights of Honor we all pledged ourselves not to do anything to cause harm to the group."

"Oh, you and your old Knights of Honor can go jump in the lake," Dwight said furiously. Turning on his heel, he stalked out of the newspaper office.

While he was helping his mother with supper, he told her what had happened.

"You know," she said, "it isn't like you to whine when you are punished for something you deserve. And certainly it is not like you to be disrespectful."

"I know, Mother." He paused. "Honestly, Mother, I don't understand what has come over me lately. I feel awful at times."

"One thing will make you feel better," she said. "Go and apologize to Mr. Howe."

"All right, I'll stop by the newspaper office when I get through work at the creamery to-morrow," Dwight promised.

The next day, as he was about to leave the creamery, Dwight saw a dirty, starved-looking fox terrier come wandering into the plant. He stood still while the little dog went sniffing from spot to spot, as though it was trying to capture a familiar scent. Every now and then, it gave a low whimper.

Dwight whistled. The dog pricked up its ears, caught sight of Dwight, and headed for the door, its tail between its legs.

Dwight called to it softly. The dog stopped, turned around, and sat down. Dwight began to coax it to come to him. For several minutes, the dog regarded him suspiciously, listening with its head cocked on one side and twitching its ear.

Dwight kept on coaxing, and finally the dog got up and walked bravely over to him.

"I'm going to get you something to eat, you poor starved thing," Dwight said, patting its head gently.

Half an hour later, Dwight walked into the newspaper office, carrying the dog in his arms.

The editor looked up from behind his desk.

"Mr. Howe, I've come to apologize about the way I behaved yesterday," said Dwight, all in one breath. "I lost my temper and said things I should not have said. So I've come to say I'm sorry and ask your pardon."

The editor looked at the boy and then at the dog. "Is that your dog?" he asked.

"Well, now he's my dog, I guess," Dwight said and laughed. "He came into the creamery, and I gave him some milk. He has stuck to me tighter than a sandburr ever since."

"He might not be a bad-looking dog after he is cleaned up and gets some meat on his ribs," said Mr. Howe. "Why are you carrying him? Is he sick or something?"

"No, sir. He's sound asleep. But he must have been wandering around lost for days. He's so tired he can't walk another step," Dwight explained. "I'm going to take him on home now."

"Well, good night, Dwight," said Mr. Howe. "And pardon is granted. You have a quick temper, and yesterday you let it get the better of you. We'll just forget about it."

"Thank you, Mr. Howe," Dwight said. "Good night, sir."

Dwight left the office and walked all the way home, carrying the sleeping dog.

CHAPTER SEVEN

Dwight Leaves Abilene

DWIGHT called the fox terrier Flip because of the way the little dog flipped one ear when he listened. Flip followed Dwight everywhere except to school. Whenever Dwight had school books under his arm, Flip would walk him as far as the corner, then trot back to the house.

Dwight found having a pet was a great deal of fun and made him feel less lonely. He taught Flip to play dead and roll over and fetch sticks. Flip grew lively and sleek.

Then Dwight found another interest to make him forget his loneliness.

The poorer boys in school did not have money to buy baseball or football uniforms. Not to wear uniforms made these boys feel as though they did not really belong to the school teams. Dwight thought there ought to be some way for everyone on the team to have a uniform.

He began to think about it. And he worked out a plan for membership and dues in an organization called The Athletic Association. All those who were not students in high school were charged admission to all the games. The Athletic Association bought uniforms and sports equipment with the money from dues and admission fees. After that, no player had to go without a uniform because he was too poor to buy one.

Other schools in Kansas heard about Dwight's plan and began to use it. Later, schools and even colleges throughout the country adopted the plan.

In June, Dwight was graduated from Garfield High School.

Edgar wrote that he was not coming home that summer. He was doing so well in school and in finding part-time work that he was staying in Ann Arbor, Michigan. As for Arthur, he was getting along fine as a messenger at the Commerce Trust Company of Kansas City. They both urged Dwight to decide upon some field of work and make plans for his education in that field.

Upon being offered a job as night supervisor at the creamery, Dwight accepted it. While he worked during the summer, he would decide what he wanted to do.

Many nights, after Dwight had checked the machines and gone his rounds at the plant, Six MacDonell and Swede Hazlett used to drop by to talk. Most of the conversation was about their plans for the future. Swede had received an appointment to the Naval Academy at Annapolis. He was wildly excited over becoming a Navy man.

"Look, Ike," he said. "Why don't you come with me? You'd make a fine naval officer. Besides, we could have a swell time together."

"Well, I don't know," Dwight answered. "Your Senator or Congressman has to recommend you for an appointment, doesn't he?"

"Of course. But you have a good school record, a fine athletic record, and everyone around here knows what a fine man your father is," Swede told him. "Those are the things that count when it comes to being recommended for an appointment."

"How about you coming along, too, Six?" Dwight asked with a grin.

"Nothing doing," said Six flatly. "I'm going to play professional baseball next year."

"Well, that's not for me," Dwight declared. "That much I know."

"There's nothing like a career in the Navy. Or the Army," Swede said. "Try for an appointment, Dwight. Go on."

"Maybe I will," Dwight told him. "Anyway, I'll think it over."

He discussed the matter later with his mother and father. Then he made an application to Senator Bristow of Kansas for an appointment. The Senator notified him that he must take an examination, prepared by the War Department, in Topeka, Kansas. If he passed that examination with high enough marks, he would be assigned to take entrance examinations later for either Annapolis or West Point.

Dwight studied as he never had studied before for the examination at Topeka. Days, during his spare time, and every free moment he had at the creamery at night, he buried his nose in a book. In October, he went to Topeka and took the examination.

"It was a very tough exam," he told Swede when he got back to Abilene. "I don't know whether I even passed it. Much less got a high mark."

"Well, anyway, you did your best," Swede

consoled him. "And you probably did better than you realize. I want to be the first to know how you came out."

An afternoon a few weeks later, Dwight went to the office where Swede worked and showed him a letter.

"Congratulations! I knew you would make it!" Swede cried, after he had finished reading. Dwight had passed with the second highest rating of the eight young men who had taken the examination. Then Swede took a second look at the letter. "But, Dwight!" he exclaimed. "Did you see? It says here that your application has been accepted all right. But you are to take the entrance exam in January for West Point. Get it, West Point! Not Annapolis."

"Yes, I know," said Dwight.

"But aren't you disappointed?" asked Swede. "I was sort of counting on you going to Annapolis with me."

"Yes, I know," Dwight repeated. "But I'm just as satisfied that it is the Army. We won't be together the way we'd planned. But the Army appeals to me."

"Landlubber!" Swede snorted, grinning at Dwight.

That evening, Dwight walked into the living room with the letter. For once, his parents were alone. They had not objected when he told them he wanted to apply for an appointment. In fact, they had helped him all they could. But they were peace-loving people. How they would feel when they knew he was so close to being in training for an Army officer?

His father sat gazing into the flames which burned brightly in the fireplace, when Dwight entered the room. His mother was playing softly on the piano. Dwight was almost sorry to break in upon them with his news.

But his mother had seen him enter. She glanced at his face, then at the letter in his hand. "You've passed," she said. "I can tell. You look all aglow."

"Yes, Mother, I did. I am to take the entrance examination for West Point in January."

"I rather thought you would do well," his father spoke up. "If you've made up your mind that a military career is what you want, I am very glad you have your appointment."

Dwight looked fondly at his father and mother. He knew how firmly they believed in settling all differences between individuals and between nations by peaceful means. Yet they could understand how it might seem right to him to be a military man. And they would never impose their own opinions on him. It was very important to them that each one of their sons should have the freedom to choose to be what he wanted to be. They were wonderful parents to have, Dwight thought.

In January, Dwight went to St. Louis where the entrance examinations for West Point were given. He passed them with high grades.

As winter passed and spring came, he began to dread leaving the town and the people he had known all his life. At last the day arrived when he was to start for West Point, and it was not dismal at all. Dwight felt far too excited to be gloomy or downcast.

He packed early. Then, whistling to Flip to follow him, he walked down to the creamery to say good-by to his father, and to Roy and Earl, who were working there now. No sooner were he and Flip inside the plant than all the workers crowded around. They congratulated Dwight and wished him good luck. He shook hands with everyone, even his father and brothers.

"We are going to miss you," they said. That was as far as they would let themselves go in expressing their feelings in public.

On the way home, Dwight stopped off to

bid good-by to some of the boys, and to Mr. Howe at the newspaper office.

Heading for home after that, Dwight's steps grew slower and slower. He sauntered along, taking a last good look at the streets and the houses and all the familiar things. Flip, who bounded on ahead, would stop occasionally to glance back at Dwight with a puzzled expression. Dwight usually walked at a pace which made Flip trot to keep up with him.

When Dwight finally reached the house, he saw his mother and Milton waiting for him on the side porch.

"Dwight, where in the world have you been?" his mother asked. "Do you realize what time it is? It's almost—"

From inside the house came the sound of the old wall clock, striking the hour.

"Good grief!" Dwight cried and flew into the house after his suitcases. He came back out with them in a moment. Setting them down, he gave his mother a big hug. Turning to Milton, he said sternly, "You take good care of Mother, you hear?"

"I sure will," Milton promised. He sniffed, and big tears started to roll down his cheeks.

[*87*]

"I'll write you right away," Dwight promised

Dwight reached down and patted Flip. "And you have to look after Flip, too, while I'm gone," he told Milton.

He picked up his suitcases.

"Let me know just as soon as you get there," his mother said.

"I'll write you right away," Dwight promised. He went down the steps and started across the yard. Flip came bounding after him.

"Hey, Milton!" Dwight called, laughing. "I thought you were going to take care of Flip."

Milton dashed out and grabbed Flip's collar. "Where do you think you're going, you old dog, you?" he scolded. "You can't follow Dwight clear to West Point."

Just then the train whistle sounded way off in the distance.

"My goodness!" exclaimed Mrs. Eisenhower. "You'll miss the train. Good-by, Dwight. Hurry!"

"Good-by! Good-by!" called Dwight and fled down the street toward the station.

CHAPTER EIGHT

West Point Cadet

As DWIGHT gazed from the window of
his quarters upon "the Point" the first day,
he thought it was one of the loveliest sights
he had ever seen. The gray stone buildings
were on a point of level land. In the back-
ground were green hills. Far up the Hudson
River, he could see the Catskill Mountains
which rose in high and rugged peaks. It was
very unlike the broad plains of Kansas which
stretched for miles upon miles.

He liked West Point, but for a short while
he was homesick. And then, all at once, he
was too busy even to think about home.

From the moment he became Cadet Eisenhower and put on his gray uniform and cap,

Dwight began to live according to strict rules. There was a time for getting up and eating and going to bed; a time for classes, study, and drill. His uniform had to be kept spotless, his buttons and shoes shined. His quarters always had to be clean and in order.

Although he did not work as hard as some of the other cadets, Dwight was a good student. He had no trouble with classes or study. His trouble was in obeying the many regulations. At home he had been used to following a few rules for most things. Here at West Point, everything had rules. And Dwight was constantly breaking some minor regulation and getting demerits.

As the months went by, he managed to collect quite a number of punishment slips, which the cadets called "slugs." Often he was forced to work off these demerits by marching for hours, back straight, head high, rifle against his shoulder. This was called a "punishment guard tour." It was very tiring, but Dwight always took it with good humor.

Although Dwight did not do too well in his studies and broke many rules, there was one thing he excelled at—football.

On a crisp day in November, he was discussing a game which the West Pointers were soon to play against the team from the Carlisle Indian School.

On the powerful Carlisle team was the great athlete, Jim Thorpe, a Sac and Fox Indian. Thorpe was considered the greatest player in football.

"If it weren't for Jim Thorpe," Dwight said to one of the other West Point players, "I think we might beat Carlisle. But that big Indian, Thorpe, has me worried."

"He's one man who has everybody worried," the player said. "We are going to have to play better football than we have ever played to beat Carlisle."

Dwight's mind was so occupied with the coming game that twice he forgot to salute, according to rules. Once, after the "lights out" signal at night, he had kept on studying in order to catch up on his lessons. With classes, study, drill, and football practice, he forgot to report himself for breaking rules.

At West Point there was an honor system. Whenever a cadet broke a rule, even if he was not caught, he was supposed to report it. Always before this, Dwight had been careful to report when he remembered breaking a rule.

By the afternoon of the Army-Carlisle game, he still had not made a report. After he was out on the field playing, it was too late.

When West Point kicked off, Big Jim Thorpe took the ball and carried it the length of the field for a touchdown. In spite of the mighty Army team's best tackling and blocking, Big Jim gained down after down for Carlisle. He never appeared to get hurt, either, in the worst pile-ups.

Dwight was in top form. His play at half-back was fast and tough. He was in there with his team, fighting for every yard of ground. The Carlisle Indians were the toughest competition Army had ever met.

It was a well-battered Army team that returned to the field after the first half. Big Jim and his Carlisle teammates seemed to Dwight to be as fresh as when they had started. Like the Garfield High School team the day it played the Kansas University freshmen, Carlisle with Big Jim Thorpe was unbeatable.

At the end of the game, Dwight went limping off the field. He had been playing so hard, he had not realized he had been hurt. The coach sent him to the doctor.

"Twisted your knee," the doctor announced, after examining it. "I am surprised it isn't worse, the way you fellows were playing out there today." He bandaged the knee and told Dwight to take care of it.

While Dwight was getting ready for supper, he noticed he had left clothes on his bed when he had gone down to the game. That was against regulations, which, in turn, reminded him of having broken several other rules.

Making sure he left his room tidy, he limped to the office to make his report.

Saluting the officer behind the desk, he said, "Cadet Eisenhower, sir. I wish to report the infraction of several rules, sir."

The officer sighed. "Two weeks without breaking any rules was too much to hope for, I suppose, Eisenhower," he said. "Proceed."

As Dwight ticked off the various things he had done, the officer looked him up and down. When he had finished, the officer asked, "You are certain you did not omit anything?"

"No, sir," replied Dwight slowly. "I don't think so, sir."

The officer was staring at Dwight's feet. Dwight glanced down quickly. Dried mud clung to the soles of his shoes.

"Oh, sir, yesterday I accidentally stepped into a mud puddle near the barracks and . . ." he began. Leaning down, he tried to flick off the mud with thumb and finger.

"Attention!" The officer's voice cracked like a whip.

Dwight straightened up and snapped to attention. "Yes, sir! I wish to add to the list, sir. My shoes are not shined as required by regulations for the proper appearance of a cadet."

"I take it that is all now," said the officer drily. Making a note on a pad of paper, he dismissed Dwight.

On his way to supper, Dwight wondered how many demerits he would get this time. None of the things he had done was really bad, he thought. Still, all the little things counted up.

He put it out of his mind during supper,

for everybody at the table was talking over the day's game. Then they went on to the game which would take place in two weeks.

"After what we went through today," one of the Army players said, "the next one should be a pushover."

As it turned out, Army won the next game easily. But Dwight hurt his knee again. This time he broke it and was sent to the hospital.

"It will take at least a month for it to mend properly," the doctor told Dwight after a careful examination.

"A month!" Dwight's heart sank. It was almost time for one of the biggest football games of the year—the Army-Navy game. "Can't I play against the Navy?" he asked.

The doctor shook his head.

"Not this year," he said. "And you'll never play again unless you are careful after you leave the hospital."

After the doctor left, Dwight's roommate came in. Seeing Dwight propped up in bed, reading, he asked, "How do you feel? You look fine."

"Oh, there's nothing the matter with me," Dwight answered casually. "Can't use my leg for a while, that's all."

His roommate grinned. "How are you at hopping on one leg?"

Dwight laughed. "Why?"

In answer, his roommate handed him a slip of paper. Dwight groaned. It was a familiar "slug." Cadet Eisenhower was sentenced to walk "six demerit and twenty-two punishment guard tours in the area within the next thirty days." That was what the last infraction of rules, which he had reported to the officer, had cost him.

"Well, this thirty days in the hospital is going to have its good points," Dwight said, waving the slip airily. "I certainly can't walk guard tours and stay in bed at the same time."

The knee mended. Dwight was released from the hospital with another warning that he must be very careful how he used it, if he wanted to be able to play football again.

Almost at once he ran into trouble.

The riding master believed in strict discipline. He also believed that cadets were often very clever at finding ways of getting out of drilling. And, for some unknown reason, he had taken a personal dislike to the young cadet from Kansas.

Dwight told him about the doctor's orders, and he asked if he could sit astride his horse during drill.

"You mean, Cadet Eisenhower, that you wish to be released from mounting and dismounting?" asked the riding master, giving Dwight a hard look.

"Yes, sir," Dwight replied. "I'm supposed to use the knee as little as possible, sir."

"Very well, if those are the doctor's orders," the officer said sourly.

So Cadet Eisenhower sat calmly on his horse while the other cadets rose and swung legs into position. The riding master kept watching Dwight suspiciously. After a while, Dwight sensed that the officer did not believe there was anything wrong with his leg. A few minutes later, he was astonished to hear himself being accused, in a loud, furious voice, of faking.

Dwight was pale as he faced the officer. He felt his hot temper rising. He was afraid to speak for fear he would say something that he would regret later.

In a sudden fury at the riding master for wrongly accusing Dwight, some of the cadets spoke up for their classmate. They were instantly silenced, and the riding master handed out demerits and punishments right and left.

"You will from now on take part in every movement of the drill," he commanded Dwight.

"Yes, sir," Dwight answered grimly, saluting.

Through the rest of the long afternoon, he mounted and dismounted, mounted and dismounted. It was all he could do to keep from crying out with the pain.

"Faint or something," whispered his friends.

"Go get the doctor. Let him explain," urged others.

Dwight shook his head. No matter how much his leg hurt, he was going through with the drill. At the end of the afternoon, Dwight's face was white and drawn. He could scarcely sit upright in his saddle. The riding master gave the last command. Dwight followed it to the letter. Then he fell from his horse. Dwight had finally collapsed. His friends carried him to the hospital. His knee was too badly hurt for him ever to play football again.

Before the end of summer, Dwight had much more important things than football to think about. There were rumors of war in Europe. There was talk that the German Kaiser was building a great army so he could conquer the nations around Germany and make himself the ruler of all Europe.

"You never can tell," Dwight's classmate, Omar Bradley, said. "The United States might be drawn into a war. We are going to have to work hard to be prepared to be officers in our Army."

Dwight really buckled down to work during his last year. He was near the bottom of a class of 277, but he raised his grades a little day by day. By Commencement Day, he had an average of 87%.

At the graduation ceremony on the West Point parade ground, he joined in singing:

"The Corps! The Corps! The Corps!
The Corps! Bareheaded salute it,
With eyes up, thanking our God
That we of the Corps are treading
Where they of the Corps have trod."

As he sang, Dwight thought of the four years he had been at "the Point," and of the many friends he had made. Soon they would be leaving for their various posts. He himself had been ordered to Texas. It was not as though he would really be separated from them, he thought. He would see many of them again sometime, somewhere. They were all Army men now.

CHAPTER NINE

Tank Men Without Tanks

FROM off in the dim gray light, Captain Eisenhower heard the bugler blow reveille. Throwing aside his blanket, he sat up and reached under the cot for his shoes. He put them on and was dressed.

There was so much work at Camp Colt, Gettysburg, Pennsylvania, that he was often too tired when he went to bed to take off his clothes. All he could manage was to tumble onto his cot by the time it was midnight.

As many people had feared, a war had broken out even before Dwight had left West Point. Soon after graduation, he had been sent to an Army post in Texas. There in San Antonio, he had met pretty Mamie Doud,

Mamie always went with him

and on a July day nearly a year later, they had been married.

Since then Eisenhower had been promoted to captain, and had been sent from one Army post to another. His young wife, Mamie, always went with him.

Meanwhile the war in Europe had spread. At last the United States joined France and England to fight against Germany, and Eisenhower had hoped to be sent overseas. Instead, the young captain had been put in command of Camp Colt and ordered to train men who would be sent to Europe to fight the enemy with tanks.

Mamie had set up housekeeping in a little cottage near the camp. She often thought she might as well have stayed in Texas, for she saw little of her husband. He spent almost all his time at the camp.

Now, on this early morning in April of 1918, Eisenhower walked across the creaky boards of the old camp building and into the make-shift kitchen.

"Good morning, Captain," said his orderly, pouring a cup of coffee for Eisenhower. "Some recruits arrived a little while ago," he went on. "Stopped to ask their way to their quarters. They were half frozen, so I made them some hot coffee. You don't mind, sir?"

"Of course I don't mind," replied Eisenhower. "Were they the men assigned to the tent at the other end of the camp?"

"Yes, sir."

"Hope we don't have a heavy rainfall before I get some new tents," said Eisenhower. "These old ones leak like sieves." Taking his cup of coffee, he stepped outside on the stoop.

"Breakfast coming up in a few minutes, Captain," the orderly said. "Corn meal mush, sir."

Eisenhower laughed. "Then I'll stick around," he said. "I could eat it three times a day when I was a kid, back home in Abilene."

Camp Colt. What a run-down, dreary place it was! There were some old buildings on the grounds, but not a quarter enough of them to house the men who kept pouring in. So tents of various shapes and sizes—anything that would give shelter—were used while new barracks were being built.

The camp was awakening. Soldiers, gathered around the wash benches outside the tents, joked and grumbled as they brushed their teeth and splashed water on their faces.

One line of men was already marching into the mess hall for breakfast.

Eisenhower was reminded that he had better check to see if the next week's food supplies had arrived. Setting his cup and saucer on the stoop, he strode across the grounds to the warehouse.

"No, Captain," the quartermaster told him. "The trucks haven't come yet. But we expect them anytime now."

"Be ready to go for emergency supplies, if they aren't here in a couple of hours," Eisenhower told him. Getting sufficient supplies for an ever-increasing number of men was another of his worries.

From the warehouse, Eisenhower went on to where the new barracks were going up. Progress was slow, for there was a lack of carpenters and other skilled workers. Men were already on the job, and Eisenhower called out greetings to them. Standing in front of an almost-finished building, he asked one of the workmen, "Think you'll have it ready for the men to move in next week?"

"We'd have it ready for you in a couple of days, Captain," answered the man, "if we had a little more help around here."

By the time he had made the rounds of the

camp, it was time for Eisenhower to instruct the men in the use of the tank, the new war weapon. He hurried to the classroom in one of the old buildings. There, with blackboard drawings and a miniature model, he showed the class the make-up of a tank and how it operated.

From there, he went out on the field and taught men how to use tanks in battle.

Captain Eisenhower did all of his teaching and training without a single tank. There were no tanks. They were waiting for tanks to come from a factory in Dayton, Ohio. No one seemed to know exactly when they would arrive. So Eisenhower taught and trained men to use something which many of them had never seen and most of them would not know at first hand until they were sent overseas.

It was past noon when Eisenhower started back to his own quarters. As he approached the barracks, he saw several wagons, loaded with lumber, and some cars and trucks parked in the road in front of the door.

"Here comes the captain now!" he heard his orderly cry.

As he hurried over, Eisenhower saw a

number of civilians begin to pile out of the cars and walk toward him. In a moment, he was surrounded.

"Well, Captain, tell us where you want this stuff put. Then give us some jobs around here, and we'll go to work," said a big, smiling man.

"Why, I know you," said Eisenhower. "You're one of—"

"Sure, I'm one of your Gettysburg neighbors. Live down the street from Mrs. Eisenhower," replied the man. "Your wife has been talking about the bad conditions out here—not enough food, no shelter for the men, lack of workers. So we all got together to give you a hand. We are all in this war together, you know, Captain."

Eisenhower was taken aback. He hardly knew what to say. "My wife—" he began.

"Sure, Captain," another one of the men spoke up. "Your wife talked around among the neighbors. Then we talked to some of the other people in town. Aroused a lot of interest in the welfare of Camp Colt. Merchants, businessmen, everybody contributed food and materials. These fellows here volunteered to do some work. Anyhow, Mrs. Eisenhower said to just come on out and see you."

Eisenhower smiled fondly, thinking of Mamie. "She sure was right," he said to the men. "I can't tell you how welcome you are. Now, if you will just follow me, I'll show you where you can take the supplies. Then I will take you to the man in charge of construction."

It was two o'clock by the time he returned to his quarters.

"I feel hungry," he said to his orderly. "I think I'd like some corn meal mush. Will it take long?"

"No, sir," replied the orderly. "I've had it ready since five o'clock this morning, Captain. I don't know whether you realize it or not, sir, but you haven't had anything but a cup of coffee since supper last night."

"Come to think of it," said Eisenhower, "I don't believe I have."

Within a few months, men trained in tank warfare were being sent from Camp Colt to Colonel Patton's outfit in France. Although no tanks had ever been used, these troops were so well trained under Eisenhower that they needed only ten days further training overseas with actual tanks before going into battle.

Captain Eisenhower had succeeded in accomplishing an almost impossible task.

He was promoted to Major and received orders from the Army to go overseas. But before he could sail, the Armistice was signed on November 11, 1918. The war was over.

There followed a number of peacetime assignments.

Eisenhower was ordered to attend Command and General Staff School at Fort Leavenworth, Kansas, where he finished at the head of his class. Next, he was sent to France to write a guide book of the battlefields of the First World War.

Next, Major Eisenhower went with General Fox Conner to Panama to set up a garrison and anti-aircraft gun emplacements. Then, with Brigadier General Douglas MacArthur, he went to the Philippines to help work out a plan of defense in case of enemy attack.

With him, in all his travels, went Mamie. Whether they were assigned to a room, an apartment, or a house, she made for her husband and their son John a real home. It was always a warm and friendly place where all the other officers were welcome. The "Club Eisenhower," the officers called it.

It was while the Eisenhowers were still in the Philippines that trouble broke out in Europe. A man named Adolf Hitler had come into power in Germany. He had built up a great and powerful army. With this army he invaded Austria, Czechoslovakia, and Poland. This caused England and France to declare war on Germany.

Then, in 1940, soon after the Eisenhowers had returned to the United States, the German armies invaded Denmark, Norway, Belgium, and Holland. Italy jumped into the fight to help Germany. Japan signed a friendly pact with Germany and Italy. The terrible war was spreading through most of the world.

It looked now as though the United States must surely be drawn into it, and preparations for war were being made in many parts of the country. American soldiers were already being trained for actual combat. One of the best ways of training soldiers is to hold

manuevers that are as much like real warfare
as possible.

In September, 1941, a big mock war was
fought in Louisiana. Eisenhower, who was
now a colonel, assisted General Kreuger, who

was in charge of one of the armies which
fought in this "war."

The top-ranking generals of the Army
went to Louisiana to observe these maneuvers. Colonel Eisenhower had done such a

fine job in planning how and where General Kreuger's army should fight that it won the mock war. This made a deep impression on the other generals. When Eisenhower returned to his post at Fort Sam Houston, in Texas, he told his wife that he had been promoted again. Now he was a brigadier general.

Of course Mamie Eisenhower was happy about this, even though it meant that her husband must now work harder than ever. She knew that he was tired, and that he was worried, too. For it looked as though the United States might soon be drawn into a war with Japan.

"But Ike and I are going to West Point to see John, this Christmas, no matter what happens," she thought one Sunday afternoon in December.

She was glad her tall young son had decided to become an army officer like his father.

"And Ike is as pleased as I am," she told herself as she sank into an easy chair in the big living room.

She was alone, for her husband had come home at noon from his office, saying that he was dead tired. He was now in his room taking a nap. Suddenly she heard the phone which was beside his bed ring loudly. It must have wakened him at once.

"Yes?" she heard him reply, and his voice sounded tense. "What? When did they do it? Yes, yes, I'll be right there."

In no time at all he came hurrying into the room, buttoning up the jacket of his uniform. His face was very grave.

"It's come," he said quietly. "The Japs have attacked our fleet at Pearl Harbor and that means war, for sure. Turn on the radio so you can keep track of what's happening. I'm on my way to my office and don't know when I'll get back."

The door slammed behind him as he ran down the steps. Mrs. Eisenhower watched him go swinging down the street. Then she twisted a radio dial. An excited announcer was broadcasting news about the attack. We would soon be at war with the Japanese, he said. And with their ally, Germany. We would fight in Europe and in Asia. Now there would be war—war—war!

There was no trip to West Point for Dwight Eisenhower that Christmas to see his son John. Within a few days, Eisenhower had received a phone call from Washington. He was ordered to leave at once for the capital and to report to General Marshall at the War Department, who would give him an important assignment.

CHAPTER TEN

New Assignment

IT WAS a hot June day. In Washington the leaves on the trees wilted under a scorching sun. But in General Marshall's blue-walled office in the War Department building, the air was cool.

Major General Dwight Eisenhower smiled as he laid a sheaf of papers on General Marshall's desk.

"I've drawn up a directive—some rules and some plans—for the man who is to take command of our forces in Europe," he said. "I know you didn't ask me for such a report, but I thought you might like to have it anyway."

He turned to leave.

"Don't go," Marshall said. "I'd like to look at this now."

He began to read through the thirty-page report. Eisenhower stepped to the window.

Absent-mindedly he watched the people in the street below. He was thinking of all that had happened since he had reached Washington the previous December.

After the attack on Pearl Harbor, the United States had quickly declared war on Japan. Then Germany and Italy had declared war on the United States. And already thousands of American men had been shipped abroad to fight.

Now the time had come to set up a head-quarters in Europe for the American overseas forces. And Dwight Eisenhower had been sent to England to discuss this matter with the top officers of the British Army.

While in London, he had discovered ways in which the Americans could best work with the British and their allies in fighting the enemy.

The report he had just given General Marshall contained suggestions which would help the man who would command the American forces abroad.

Marshall glanced through its pages. Then he swung around in his chair to face Eisenhower. "Does this directive suit *you?*" he asked. "Are you satisfied with it?"

"Yes, sir. I've given it a lot of thought," replied Eisenhower. "I think it's pretty complete. Of course, you may have suggestions or corrections that you want to make."

"I'm glad it suits you," Marshall said, looking directly at Eisenhower. "Because you are the man who will be working under this directive. You are being placed in command of the European Theater. You are to leave for London next week."

[*119*]

"Me?" Eisenhower was taken completely by surprise. To be in command of all the American forces in Europe! He had dreamed sometimes about getting such an assignment, but he had never really believed that his dream would come true. Now he was almost speechless. And before long he was hurrying home to tell his wife the good news.

"I'm going to be in command of the whole shebang," he told her. "Marshall's given me command of all of our troops in Europe."

After dinner in their apartment, the Friday night before he left, he poked his head in the door of the bedroom where Mamie was busily packing his trunk and suitcases. "I'll be in the study," he said. "I've got some work to do. And I want to phone Mother."

"Don't forget, Milton and Helen will be over later," Mamie said. "You'll want to see them."

"Of course," Dwight said. "By the way, when Johnny called from West Point did he say what time he was arriving in the morning?"

"No. He just said he was catching the first train," Mamie told Dwight. "Give your mother my love when you call."

"I will." Eisenhower went to his study and

called his mother on long distance. He told her that he was leaving for his new job.

"God bless you and your work," she said. There was a pause before she went on. "It seems strange to have all of you boys so far away. When your father was alive it was different. But now this old house seems so big and quiet and empty."

Dwight sat for a moment after he had said good-by, thinking sadly of his mother's loneliness. Then, pulling his briefcase toward him, he opened it and took out the papers on which he still had to do some work.

"I'll never in the world be able to close your trunk," Mamie called from the other room.

"Mickey McKeogh is coming over to take the stuff to the plane tomorrow," Dwight said. "We'll have him jump on the trunk. That will close it all right."

"And squash your clothes at the same time," Mamie told him, laughing.

"I'm taking Mickey with me, you know," Dwight said.

"Of course. It would break his heart if you didn't," Mamie said.

She smiled as she thought of Sergeant Michael McKeogh. Mickey had been her husband's orderly for a long time and was devoted to him.

In his study Eisenhower was already looking over a copy of the report he had given General Marshall.

"I must see to it that there is no jealousy between the Army, Navy, and Air Forces," he thought. "They must work together as a team. The English and Americans must form a team, too. Neither must be allowed to feel better than the other."

He leaned back in his chair, still planning. The Germans had invaded North Africa and the English were fighting there, trying to drive them out. Help must be sent to the English forces as quickly as possible. And, once the Germans were thrown out of North Africa there would have to be a plan for landing on . . .

The ringing of the doorbell interrupted his train of thought.

"That's Milton and Helen," Mamie called.

Dwight slipped the papers back into his briefcase and locked it.

That evening, he and Milton discussed many things. And it was late when his brother and sister-in-law left. But Dwight was very glad to have had a last visit with Milton.

A deep understanding had developed between the two brothers. They liked to discuss their problems, for they always found they could help each other.

Next morning, John, looking trim in his gray cadet's uniform, arrived in time for breakfast. Eisenhower put aside the problems and worries about the job which lay ahead and enjoyed talking with his son about West Point.

When Sunday afternoon came, John had to return to the Academy. He stood with his mother and father for a moment at the top of the front steps. Then, giving his mother a quick hug, he turned and held out his hand to his father. There was a firm handclasp.

"Good-by, Johnny."

"Good luck, Dad."

Dwight and Mamie watched their son stride off. When John reached the sidewalk, he whirled about. Snapping to attention, his hand flashed up in a clean, sharp salute.

Eisenhower smiled proudly. Then he, too, came to attention and returned his son's salute.

The very next day Major General Dwight D. Eisenhower boarded a plane for England to tackle the biggest job he had ever had.

CHAPTER ELEVEN
Operation Torch

GENERAL EISENHOWER sat at his big desk in his headquarters at 20 Grosvenor Square. This was only his second day in London, yet already he had held several important meetings with different members of his staff.

"This is a tough war we are fighting," he had told them. "But I don't want anyone working with me who isn't sure we're going to win it. And anyone who isn't prepared to work hard had better find himself another job quickly. Solve your own problems whenever you can, but remember, I'll always be ready to help you when you need me."

Now, as the last group of officers left the room, Eisenhower smiled.

"I have a staff of fine men," he thought,

"and I think they're going to make a good team."

He reached for a sheaf of papers and called his secretary in from the next room. He had so much to do, he hardly knew where to begin.

Not only must he make plans for an attack on the enemy, but he must build up an understanding between the Americans and the English, and show them how they could work and fight together.

All the rest of that day and during the weeks that followed, he was busier than he had ever been before. He held many meetings with high-ranking officers, both British and American. He inspected air bases and supply centers. He dictated reports to President Roosevelt and General Marshall in the United States. He called on King George in Buckingham Palace, to pay his respects. He spent a night with Winston Churchill, and before he left he and the British Prime Minister had become good friends.

Wherever he went, people liked and trusted him. After a little speech which he made in a club one day, an old English woman approached him.

"I've lost my husband and my son in this war," she told him. "Until today I thought we

[*125*]

were going to lose the war, too. Now I've heard you speak and I'm sure we'll win it."

Eisenhower worked so hard that when night came he was worn out. Once he slept right through an air raid, though German planes were flying low over London, and anti-aircraft guns were chattering in Hyde Park, just across the street from the hotel where he was staying.

There were many air raids on England that summer, and across the English Channel there was bitter fighting. In North Africa, too, the English were still battling with the Germans. It was there that General Eisenhower and his British and American advisers decided to make the first large-scale attack.

One hot July day, the general explained this decision and the plan of attack to some of his officers. It was very quiet in the big room in London where the meeting was being held. All the men's eyes were on Eisenhower as he stood before a map of Africa, hanging on the wall.

Holding a pointer in his hand, he began, "Gentlemen, ships will come from Europe and the United States. They will strike at these places along the northern coast of Africa." Eisenhower touched the three different ports marked on the map. "They will all strike at the same time."

There was a murmur of agreement among the men. "Yes, yes, we see," several said enthusiastically.

"One large group of ships will come from the United States bringing the American First Army," continued Eisenhower. "This army will lead the attack on the western part of the front." He moved his pointer over to the west of the African coast. "Right here," he said, "at a place called Casablanca."

"But how will you land the soldiers?" asked one man. "Casablanca is protected by enemy guns and troops."

"Landings will be supported by aircraft," replied Eisenhower. "Planes will fly over, destroying gun batteries. They will fight off the enemy while the troops are landing."

As Eisenhower went on with the details of the invasion, the men grew more and more enthusiastic.

The British already had General Rommel, the brilliant commander of the German Army, on the run.

"By striking with all the forces of land and sea and air," Eisenhower said, "the invasion may well be successful. But speed and surprise are all-important."

Before the meeting broke up, all were

"Landings will be supported by aircraft,"
Eisenhower replied

agreed that the plan for attack on North Africa was a fine one. And if anyone could make it work, Eisenhower was that man.

Meanwhile Eisenhower was waiting for President Roosevelt, Prime Minister Churchill, and others to approve his plan, which had been given the code name "Torch." He knew that they would also select a man to be the Allied Commander-in-Chief of the British and American Armies.

No one was surprised when Eisenhower was chosen to fill that important post.

"How do you feel, Ike, now that you're a four-star general?" Harry Butcher asked as the two men dined together, the day the news was received.

"Haven't had time to think about it," Eisenhower replied with a grin. "Torch! That's what's on my mind. Is the plan going to work?"

He laid down his fork as a truck roared by in the street outside. "It certainly is noisy!" he said. "Are you still trying to find us a quiet place in the country, Harry, so we can get away now and then?"

"Still trying," Butcher replied. He had been looking for several weeks for a place he thought the general would like. It was not until almost the end of August that he found it.

Telegraph Cottage was set among tall trees, with a velvety lawn and a rose garden. In the hedgerows, bees hummed and birds sang. There was even a vegetable garden, from which Mickey McKeogh delightedly served the general corn on the cob.

Perhaps it was the homelike atmosphere of Telegraph Cottage that made Eisenhower suddenly announce that he wanted a dog. So, as a birthday present, his office staff gave him a sturdy four-months-old Scottie puppy. The puppy had shining, mischievous eyes and a proud little strut. Eisenhower named him Telek.

"That sounds like a trade name for a toothbrush," Harry Butcher remarked.

"Well, his tail looks like a toothbrush," the general said.

Telek went everywhere with General Ike, though he had to wait outside in the car when Eisenhower went to say good-by to King George VI.

The time at last had come for action. Torch had been approved by President Roosevelt and Prime Minister Churchill, and the date had been set for the invasion. It had a code name, too—D-Day, November 8th.

On November 4th, General Eisenhower left England in a Flying Fortress for the Rock of Gibraltar, where his new headquarters would be. It was absolutely necessary that enemy

spies should not learn of his plans. So, in British and American newspapers, a story had been published that the general had been re-called to Washington, to account for his departure from London. Ike wished he could let Mamie know the truth, but secrecy was vital and he dared not risk sending her a message.

Eisenhower's new headquarters had been cut out of solid rock. A long, damp, limestone tunnel led to air-conditioned offices fourteen hundred feet down. There the general and his staff worked throughout the two anxious days before D-Day, H-Hour.

This was the hardest time of all for Eisenhower. Would the weather and surf be rough? Had the secret messages about Torch been decoded by the enemy? *Nothing* must go wrong. Like a football team, the members of the Allied team had to fight together to give the enemy swift, crushing blows.

About five-thirty in the afternoon of November 7th, Eisenhower sent a message to all the Torch forces:

WARNING ORDER. H-HOUR CONFIRMED NOVEMBER 8. FOR EAST AND CENTER 1 A.M. FOR WEST ABOUT 4:30 A.M.

Nobody got much sleep inside the Rock that night. General Ike and his staff paced the floor, drinking coffee and listening to intercepted code radio messages sent from aircraft carriers creeping toward the African coast.

And the messages brought good news. While American bombers circled overhead, thousands of American and British soldiers were being landed on the beaches.

The attack came as a complete surprise to the Germans and their friends. Much damage was done before they could recover from their surprise and prepare to fight back. Then they started to fire the guns in their pillboxes along the waterfront. The battle was on.

Another squadron of American planes

roared overhead. This time, bombs were dropped on enemy ships, submarines, and oil tankers in the harbor. A U. S. battleship with her destroyers was moving in, firing broadside after broadside into the enemy ships outside the harbor.

By dawn, messages received said that Operation Torch was proceeding on schedule. General Eisenhower, exhausted but relieved, went and splashed cold water on his face. "Before long," he thought, "this news will be broadcast on the radio at home. Then Mamie will know where I am."

All that day the bombers continued the attack over Casablanca, Oran, and other spots along the coast. The enemy fought back with planes, shore batteries, and guns on battleships. But American and British ships were landing troops in spite of the resistance.

By the next day, American forces, supported by the British, under the command of General Eisenhower had successfully landed in North Africa. And the invasion was underway.

Week after week, month after month, the battle for North Africa went on. By the middle of May, 1943, with the French, English, and Americans, the Army, Navy, and Air Force all fighting together as one huge team under

Eisenhower, the Germans were driven out of the country.

For months Eisenhower had been working at top speed. He got little rest. He often was too busy to eat.

When General George Marshall visited him at his new headquarters in Algiers, he was shocked by Eisenhower's wasted appearance.

"You are to get some proper food and rest," Marshall told him. As he saw Eisenhower start to protest, he added in a severe tone, "That's an order."

"Yes, sir," said Eisenhower solemnly. "I will do my best, sir, to carry out your orders."

"We can't have you getting sick," grumbled Marshall. "You are too important to our cause."

At Algiers, Eisenhower did try to live more normally. Since Operation Torch had been so highly successful, he could quit driving himself so hard. He even found a little time for recreation.

Yet his work had to go on. And, although North Africa had just been taken, Eisenhower was already planning the next campaign. The clearing of North Africa was only the first step to a much more important invasion.

CHAPTER TWELVE

Step by Step

THE next important step in the plan was the capture of the island of Sicily. Every detail of the attack was worked out carefully.

On July 10, the Americans and the British made their first landing. Troops began piling out of the landing craft, only to be met by a barrage from the German and Italian guns. Men made a dash for the beach and flung themselves down to escape the enemy fire.

More craft put more American troops ashore. On another part of the beach, British troops started to land. The British were met by German and Italian gunfire. And enemy troops came at them in a great onrush.

Allied planes, trying to drop bombs over

enemy gun batteries, were caught in the fire of anti-aircraft guns. Some of the planes fell to earth in flames.

In the war room, Eisenhower was in touch by radio with the men on the shore. The messages were discouraging. The Germans and Italians were putting up a stiff fight to keep the British and Americans from getting a foothold on the beach.

All the ships, except the destroyers in the Allied fleet, had moved in close to shore. The destroyers had been cruising at some distance away.

Now came the order for all the destroyers to move in closer.

The destroyers drew nearer to land. As soon as they were within range of the enemy, they began firing. The Germans and Italians had not expected more ships and men and guns. To the dismay of the enemy, the destroyers kept passing the beach, with their guns blasting away. The Germans and Italians fought back desperately, but they could not withstand the heavy gunfire.

Before long the Italians began to retreat. Then the Germans fell back. American and

British troops flowed across the beaches and up the banks and ridges after the retreating enemy.

Eisenhower's carefully planned teamwork between air, land, and sea forces had won the battle. Soon after this, the Italians surrendered and signed an armistice, promising that they would fight no more. Now the Allies were ready to move on to Salerno.

Eisenhower chose a close friend, General Mark Clark, to command the Salerno operation. Both he and Clark knew that to estab-

lish a beachhead at Salerno would be a real test of American and British forces. There were nineteen tough German divisions in Italy. And the city and harbor of Salerno had been so well fortified that they thought it could not be taken.

At three-thirty in the morning when the first landing craft began to nose onto the Salerno beaches, the American and British troops knew at once they were playing in the major leagues. The Germans threw up flares which lighted the whole beach. Then guns from the hilltop opened up.

Many men were wounded. Many others were drowned. More men came on, only to meet a criss-cross of machine-gun fire. Still the troops came on.

German planes flew overhead with their guns chattering. American and British fighter planes engaged the Germans in a battle in the air, while the infantry kept coming in waves onto the beaches.

When the sun came up, it shone upon American and British troops so mixed together that they made one great army. Side by side, the Americans and the British dug in to hold the beach. But could they hold it?

In Algiers, Ike faced his staff. "The beach-head can be saved only if General Montgomery can get there fast," he told them.

General Bernard Montgomery was the British general who had been with Eisenhower in North Africa.

"And we must get better air protection," continued Eisenhower. "Otherwise, our boys, instead of trapping the Germans, will be trapped themselves."

However, within the next few days, General Montgomery advanced rapidly and made contact with the American Fifth Army patrols. The two Allied forces joined. The beachhead was saved.

This was the beginning of a long struggle to conquer Italy. Although his staff thought he should not take what seemed to them unnecessary risks, Eisenhower often visited the troops in the fighting areas.

These were grim days for Eisenhower. He needed the encouragement the soldiers could give him. He wondered many times if the great slaughter of men which was going on day after day could possibly be right. He thought of his grandfather and of his mother and father, and their love for peaceful ways.

He knew the great value they had always placed on human life.

He remembered his mother saying that there must be some reason why he should want to enter the Army. And he must have felt that joining the Army was the right thing to do. Now, sometimes, he felt unsure.

His inner struggle gave him a feeling of great loneliness. To overcome it, he was with the men as often as possible.

"According to the textbooks," he said in a talk to them one time, "a commander should meet and talk with his troops in order to inspire them. For my part, I need to draw my inspiration from you."

His men sensed his loneliness. They knew he was not just making speeches. They cheered him until they were hoarse. And they showed in every way possible that they were as proud of him as he was of them. They inspired him to go on being the best commander he knew how to be.

From the beachhead at Salerno, it was to take Allied troops twenty long months to march to Rome. The Germans continued to fight all the way. But Italy was at last conquered, and Rome fell into Allied hands.

Meanwhile, in November of 1943, a big meeting of the heads of all the Allied nations, except the Soviet Union, was held in Cairo, Egypt. Eisenhower went there to meet with President Roosevelt of the United States and

Prime Minister Churchill of Great Britain. Since the Chinese Nationalists were helping to fight in the war in Asia against Japan, Generalissimo Chiang Kai-shek was there, too.

[*143*]

Although it was November, the weather was warm in Cairo. On the terrace in the sun, Eisenhower sat and discussed the next step in the plan for defeating the Germans. This step was the invasion of France, to take that country out of enemy hands. Then the Allies could march on Germany itself.

Puffing upon his cigar, Churchill explained how Allied troops could be collected along the coast of England, directly across the Channel from France.

Roosevelt, who had always made the Navy one of his great interests, talked about the way troops would be transported across the Channel by ships and boats and special barges.

Chiang Kai-shek listened, for the most part, his face calm but his eyes bright and alert.

Back and forth the discussion went between Eisenhower and the others until all understood clearly just how the invasion would be launched.

"Now," said Eisenhower, "we come to a most important point. The armed forces of the Allied nations are going to make the invasion. But how are they going to work together?"

A smile came over Churchill's ruddy face.

[*144*]

"No doubt you have some ideas about that, yourself, General," he said.

Roosevelt settled back in his chair and said, "Yes, General, let's hear what you have to say, first."

"Mr. President," Eisenhower said, "if the invasion of France is to be successful, and if the final defeat of the Germans is to be successful also, then the armies, navies, and air forces of the Allies must continue to work together as a single team." Then he went on to explain why this was so. And he pointed out that a team needed a captain, so that all the members of the team could work together.

Roosevelt, Churchill, and Chiang Kai-shek listened attentively to him. And they all agreed with him.

On the last day of the conference, General Marshall handed Eisenhower a folded slip of paper. Opening it, Eisenhower read the note. A Supreme Headquarters of the Allied Expeditionary Forces of Great Britain, the United States, France, the Soviet Union, and China was to be set up in London. General Dwight D. Eisenhower had been chosen unanimously to be the Supreme Commander of the Allied Expeditionary Forces. On the

He had been chosen to be the Supreme Commander

note were the initials of the President of the United States and the Prime Minister of Great Britain.

Supreme Commander! Although Ike was deeply honored, he could not help chuckling a bit at such a high-sounding title. Then he was immediately serious. The title told him what a lonely job lay ahead. He alone would be held responsible for many decisions. And he would have to make many decisions that he knew he would dread making.

CHAPTER THIRTEEN

Operation Overlord

Before he took up his heavy task as Supreme Commander of Operation Overlord, as it was called, something happened to make Eisenhower very happy. He was given a twenty-day leave, top secret. He was as excited about it as a boy.

With Harry Butcher, Mickey McKeogh, and two Scottie puppies, Ike flew to the United States.

Harry Butcher's wife lived across the hall from Mrs. Eisenhower's apartment in the Wardman Park Hotel in Washington, D. C. About two o'clock on the morning of January 2nd, both women heard the sound of hushed, but familiar laughter in the hall.

Mamie rushed to the door and threw it open. Mrs. Butcher opened her door at the same moment.

The next instant, she and Mamie were being hugged by their husbands. The Scottie puppies, which had been brought for Milton's children and Harry's daughter, jumped about, barking noisily.

"Quick! Come inside and shut the door!" the Supreme Commander ordered anxiously. "The hotel doesn't allow dogs in the apartments."

Mamie couldn't help laughing as she closed the door. Imagine the Supreme Commander of the Allied Forces being afraid of the manager of a hotel!

It was a joyful meeting. Two days later she and Ike went to West Point to visit John. Then Ike flew to Manhattan, Kansas, to see Milton, who was now president of Kansas State University. Ike very much wanted a family reunion in Abilene, but it would have been impossible to keep his visit a secret. And it had to be kept secret for fear information concerning Eisenhower's whereabouts might leak out to the enemy.

At Milton's, however, there were Ike's mother and Arthur and his family. So it was a sort of reunion and a happy one although Edgar and Earl could not attend. And gay, chubby Roy had died suddenly two years before.

The twenty days passed much too quickly. Soon Eisenhower was back in England. He spent the next six months working on plans for Operation Overlord. During that time troops, war matériels, and equipment were brought together in England. Planes, ammunition, tanks, food—these and many more things had to be in readiness. Ships, boats, barges, and other craft had to be collected in the various English ports. Everything had to be got ready for the invasion of France.

One of the ways in which Eisenhower prepared the troops for this invasion was to have them practice in a mock war. From his own experience on maneuvers in Louisiana swamps years ago, he knew the great value of practice warfare.

He selected Slapton Sands on the southwest coast of England as the best place for the maneuvers. There was a great stretch of beach and high cliffs from which he could watch the make-believe attack. Also, the place was quite like the French coast upon which the real attack would be made later.

Eisenhower had the troops divided into two sides. One side was to try to keep the other side from landing on the Cornwall beach. The men who were to be the invaders were ordered to the boats. The other men, the defenders, took up their positions on shore, prepared to keep the invaders off.

Eisenhower ordered the battle to begin. Then he watched the two sides battle for possession of the beach. As soon as a group of men would try to land from the boats, the men on the beach would try to drive them back. Eisenhower observed their actions very carefully.

From this mock war, he had discovered what he needed to know before sending men into real combat.

Now a time was decided upon for crossing the English Channel and making an attack upon the French coast. It was to take place between June 2 and June 10.

Already ships, destroyers, mine-sweepers, and gunboats had assembled in the English Channel and off the coast of Spain. The Russians were waiting for the D-Day signal to move in from the east toward Berlin. Everything was going according to plan. Everyone would be ready.

Eisenhower now set up headquarters in a trailer which he called his "circus wagon." It was moved to a place called Southwick Park, near Portsmouth, and set up in the woods there. From the near-by beaches the attack would be launched. The invasion was finally set for June 5.

Then on Saturday, June 3, came a shattering blow.

The entire staff met at Eisenhower's trailer headquarters in the woods at four o'clock in the morning to hear the weather report. High winds and rough seas were developing. The weather would be very bad on June 5. It might be better on the sixth, but again it might not. The long-range forecast was not favorable.

Everyone looked at Eisenhower. His face was grim. "We'll postpone the invasion for twenty-four hours," he said. "We'll meet here at four tomorrow morning."

Before dawn the following day, they all met again and listened as three weather experts made their forecasts. Tuesday, June 6, would be windy. The ceiling would be clear by noon. By afternoon the wind would die down for a few hours. Beyond that, the weather looked very bad.

"I know Montgomery and Omar Bradley and George Patton can move the ground forces in almost any kind of weather," Eisenhower said. "So it's pretty much up to Ramsay of sea operations and Leigh-Mallory of air."

"I'll chance it," said Leigh-Mallory, the British Air Commander.

"If the Air thinks he can do it, the Navy certainly can," Ramsay declared.

Ike got up and paced the small space between his desk and the wall. He began to speak, almost as if he were thinking out loud.

"Some soldier once said that the weather is always neutral," he said quietly. "Nothing could be more untrue. Bad weather is always the enemy of the attacker. We are the attackers in this invasion. The troops are all keyed up. They may never get that fine-edge sharpness again. The bad weather is due to last for weeks. Any long wait before the attack, and information about our plans might leak out. If we lose the element of surprise, we will quite possibly lose the war."

He continued pacing the floor in silence. Although they could give him their sympathy, his staff could not help him. It was up to him alone to make the decision. He made it very quietly and simply, without even looking up.

"All right," he said. "We move at seven o'clock in the morning."

The officers hurried to their posts. They all had last-minute commands to issue.

Eisenhower sank into his chair. Tomorrow he would supervise the take-off and bid Godspeed to the troops. Until then . . .

"Mickey!" he called. "Get me the car. I'm going to drive out to the airfields. I have to see the boys of the 82nd and 101st Airborne."

Mickey fetched the car and Eisenhower drove quickly to the first field. When he arrived, he found four staff photographers there, wanting to take pictures of him and the airmen.

"Get out!" Eisenhower ordered them.

"But, sir—"

"Out!!"

Ike knew there were other generals who might think photos of the Supreme Commander bidding good-by to the "Suicide Club," as the fliers were called, would be inspiring. To Ike, it seemed like taking pictures of men condemned to die.

The men stood at ease beside their planes. Alone, Ike walked slowly past the long, long lines of boys. Often he stopped to talk with one or another of them.

"Where you from?" Ike would ask.

"Utah, sir."

"Raise wheat?"

"Yes, sir."

"How many bushels per acre?" Ike asked.

"Not enough."

"Better luck this harvest." Then Ike would go on and ask another man, "Where you from?"

"Kansas, sir."

"Where in Kansas?"

"Manhattan, sir."

"That's not far from my home town," Eisenhower would say.

"I know, sir. Abilene."

It was evening by the time Ike had visited the last airfield. He stood watching as the men were ordered into their planes. Then he climbed to the roof of headquarters building. He stood there as plane after plane wheeled out of the line-up, and echelon after echelon sped down the runways and swept up and westward toward the distant coast of France.

He lifted his hand to the visor of his cap and held the salute until the last plane was out of sight.

As he climbed down from the roof, Ike glanced at the windsock on top of the Weather Building. It was flying straight out.

"Twenty-five miles per hour and building

*He stood watching as the men were ordered
into their planes*

to gale velocity," one of the weather men told Ike.

"Not good," he said, his lips tightening. Going to his car, he asked the driver to take him to the sea cliffs.

There, he peered through the fog at the waters below. He knew the Channel was filled with every sort of craft, but all he could see were dark masses on the water.

He returned to headquarters.

At midnight the wind increased. At four o'clock, it was blowing thirty miles an hour. By six, the wind had hit forty miles. At six-thirty, it had dropped to thirty.

A short time later that morning, the people of the conquered countries in Europe took new hope as they heard a strong, calm voice come over the radio. It was General Eisenhower, making his invasion broadcast:

"People of western Europe! A landing was made this morning on the coast of France by troops of the Allied Expeditionary Force . . . the hour of your liberation is approaching . . ."

In America, at one o'clock in the afternoon of June 6, Cadet John Eisenhower stood with his mother and some friends outside the chapel at West Point. He was about to go in with the others of his class to receive his diploma.

All of a sudden there was a disturbance in in the crowd. Reporters and photographers pushed their way toward the chapel.

"Just step this way a little, will you, Eisenhower?" said a photographer.

"You, too, Mamie," another said.

"Please, not now," John begged.

"Only take a minute," the first photographer told him.

Reluctantly, John and Mamie posed together.

"We had hoped this would be John's day," Mamie said. "John is the one who is graduating."

"But his father has just pulled off the greatest invasion in history," shouted one of the reporters.

"What!" Mamie's jaw dropped.

John's mouth opened in surprise. Then mother and son hugged each other in happy pride and relief. The photographers took their pictures just at that moment.

Then the reporters told them that assault troops had landed in France. The invasion was underway. The news had been broadcast by Ike himself.

In the weeks that followed, the armies of the Allies drove on toward Germany. The plan which Eisenhower had worked out so carefully was successful.

Germany surrendered on May 7, 1945, and the war in Europe was over.

CHAPTER FOURTEEN
Home Again

THE town of Abilene had spent weeks pre-
paring floats for a big pageant. Now the day
of the big celebration had arrived. With banners and flags streaming in the wind and the
band playing, the floats passed slowly through
the main streets. There were floats showing
cowboys and Indians, trail drivers, and people of the early days in Abilene. There were
others which showed events in the life of
General Dwight D. Eisenhower.

This was the day the whole town was cele-
brating the return of its great military hero.

In the parade, riding in an open car, were
Ike and Mamie. As they rode through Abilene's streets between crowds of shouting

people, General Ike waved his arms and grinned genially at them all. Mamie smiled at the excited citizens who were chanting, "Ike! Ike! Ike!"

And Eisenhower was reminded of his arrival at the National Airdrome in Washington,

when he returned after the surrender of Germany. There, more than 30,000 people had rushed out upon the great airfield to greet him. And they too had been chanting, "Ike! Ike! Ike! Ike!"

There had followed a parade through the streets to the Pentagon Building. And he had waved at the welcoming crowds while ticker tape streamed down on him from the windows of office buildings.

Then he had gone on to New York, where four million people in gay carnival spirit had showered him with confetti.

From there he had flown to Kansas City, where he was met by Mamie, who had come on ahead by train.

And everywhere he had gone, it was, "Ike! Ike! Ike!"

Then, together with their wives, Dwight's four brothers had joined him to take the train to Abilene. It had been a joyful and gay journey.

Now all these events raced through Eisenhower's mind as he waved and called greetings to the people of his home town. He was happy to think that he was being welcomed with so much friendliness.

But there were sad thoughts that came to Eisenhower at the same time. The horrors of the war were too fresh in his mind for him to be truly happy. He had seen too many wounded and dying men. Too many starving women and children. Too many homes destroyed by bombs and shell-fire. All the ticker tape, confetti, and cheering in the world could not make him forget those scenes.

However, he shoved the memories to the back of his mind as the last float of the pageant appeared. On this float were some of Eisenhower's boyhood friends, members of his old Garfield High School football team. Eisenhower waved again and again at the merry faces of Bud Hoffman, Swede Hazlett, a Navy captain now, and Wes Merryfield.

Later, in a speech he made especially to his old friends, he spoke of his father and mother as "the two really great members of the Eisenhower family."

And the keynote of most of his speeches was that we must work together as hard for peace as we have worked for war.

When Eisenhower returned to Washington, he found it difficult to settle down to the desk job of Chief of Staff of the Army. It was a great let-down after the excitement of the war. He was restless.

As Chief of Staff he made a tour of duty of the United States. He also visited Canada, Mexico, Panama, Hawaii, Japan, China, Korea, Brazil, and many countries in Europe. Between journeys, he and Mamie lived quietly at Fort Myer, Virginia.

In spite of the great interest Ike took in his work as head of the Army, Mamie realized that he was discontented.

One evening he came in with a great stack of books from the library.

"My, what do you have there?" Mamie asked him, a twinkle in her blue eyes. "Looks as if you were studying for an examination."

"Oh, nothing like that," he told her, giving her a quick kiss. "I'm just going to do some reading."

"Anything special?" she asked. As he put the books down on the table in the living room, she went over and peered at the titles. "Mmmm. They're all history books. I know you have always liked history, but why this sudden—"

"Because," Dwight interrupted, "I think I ought to do some real studying. Try to improve my education."

"Why, of course," Mamie said. "I think it is fine if you can take an interest in history. Maybe if you find a sort of hobby like that, you won't feel so restless."

Eisenhower went on with his reading of history for quite some time. Then one morning at the breakfast table he announced,

"You know, Mamie, I think it might be a good idea for me to get out of the Army. I just don't think I'm being of real service to my country any more."

"Oh dear," Mamie said, "I thought with your interest in studying and the work you are doing at the office, you were much more satisfied."

"No, Mamie," he answered. "The truth is I'm not. I have just about decided the best thing for me to do is to go teach in a small boys' school somewhere. I believe I would feel I was being truly useful."

Mamie smiled at him fondly. "I don't know what to say," she told him. "I only know that whatever you do will be right. And I shall be happy, whatever you decide."

Not long after this, Eisenhower was asked to become the president of Columbia University. He felt honored to be offered such a position. But he also felt that the president of a great university should be a scholar, not a soldier like himself. However, he was finally persuaded to accept the post.

"The first project I am going to start," he told Mamie, "is the study of war. Students should learn about the many different causes

[*167*]

of war. They ought to find out about the terrible effects of wars upon people's minds and spirits. They should see how wars keep people living in backward conditions and prevent them from leading better, more comfortable lives."

"What would you call a project like that?" Mamie asked. "I have never heard of one like it."

"It isn't exactly a new idea with me," her husband told her. "I've been thinking about it for a long time, and I have a name for it already. I'd like to call it the Institute of War and Peace Studies."

He paused for a minute. Then he went on. "There's another project I have in mind," he said. "I'd like to start a nutrition center, where young men and women can learn all about food."

Seeing Mrs. Eisenhower begin to smile, he added quickly, "No, I don't mean just planning meals and cooking. I mean learning about where certain food plants can best be grown. Why some foods contain more nourishment than others. And even how we can get new kinds of food out of the ocean."

When Eisenhower took his office as president of Columbia he did start his two projects—the Institute of War and Peace Studies, and the Nutrition Center.

There were other studies which he introduced during the two years he served as president, but these two were the most important.

In fact, Eisenhower had begun to be very interested in his new work. And he and Mamie had just begun to feel permanently settled in their new home on Morningside Heights in New York City when once again Ike had to put on his uniform.

In December, 1950, President Harry Truman asked him to be Supreme Commander of the armies of several allied countries in Europe. Eisenhower's job was to form an international fighting force, made up of men from nations in the North Atlantic Treaty Organization, or NATO as it was commonly called.

So, once more, Eisenhower set out for Europe. He began his new work in the newly built headquarters near the little village of Rocquencourt in France, not far from Paris.

Outside the new buildings in Rocquencourt flew the twelve flags of the NATO nations—the United States, Canada, Great Britain, France, Italy, Belgium, Denmark, Norway, Iceland, the Netherlands, Luxembourg, and Portugal. As other nations, such as Greece and Turkey, joined NATO later, their flags were added to the great display.

Inside the new buildings were the offices of the men who represented those nations.

All the nations had pledged themselves to work together to defend and keep peace, security, and freedom in "the North Atlantic Community." As Supreme Commander, Eisenhower worked to organize a military team that would try as hard to keep peace in the

[*170*]

world as the team of Allied nations had fought to win World War II.

No sooner, though, had he taken over his job than Congressmen from the United States began to call on him. They all wanted one thing. They wanted General Dwight D. Eisenhower to run for the office of President of the United States. Even while he had been at Columbia University, various important men in politics had tried to persuade him to enter his name as a candidate for the nomination of President. But he had always refused.

And now, when the Congressmen urged him to come home, he told them he could not. He had a job to do—a job he considered of greatest importance to the freedom of the world. He could not leave it.

CHAPTER FIFTEEN

Mr. President

ΙT WAS June 1, 1952. Eisenhower had just left President Harry Truman's office in Washington, D. C. He had reported to the President on his last tour of duty as Supreme Allied Commander, Europe. And now he was free to set out on a new career—a career in politics.

As Eisenhower walked down the steps of the White House and turned toward home, he thought back to the different people and events that gradually made him decide to run for President of the United States.

First, there had been the Congressmen who had urged him to run. Next, a "Draft Eisenhower" movement had been formed at a meeting between Governor Thomas E. Dewey of New York and several United States Senators. Then twenty-four great daily newspapers over the country endorsed him.

Finally, from the House of Representatives in Washington, letters had come advising him to run for very good reasons. "That will be the best way to be sure your efforts in Europe are not wasted," said the letters. "The surest way to promote peace in the world would be for you to be elected President."

Everywhere people were clamoring for Eisenhower. He had to make a decision.

After long and careful thought, he had written Milton. There was "one underlying principle that I have always believed to be binding on every American," he wrote. "This principle is that every citizen is required to do his duty for the country no matter what it may be."

Clearly the people of his country were calling him to still another duty. And Eisenhower realized at last that he must answer that call.

Now, opening the door of the apartment in the hotel where he and Mamie were living, he called out, "Mamie! we had better start digging out that suit of clothes I wore at Columbia University. I'll soon be a civilian."

The next day, after thirty-seven years, Ike retired from the Army. He was supposed to receive retirement pay of over $19,000 a year, but he gave that up. He was going to run for the nomination, just like any other citizen. If he accepted money from the government, even though he was entitled to it, he would not feel free and independent.

Two days after his retirement, he and Mamie started out on a campaign tour of the country. Their first stop was at Abilene. There, in his old home town, Eisenhower made his first political speech.

All of his old friends greeted him with, "Hi, Ike!"

And some of them added, "We got so used to seeing you in a uniform, you looked strange there for a minute in those civilian clothes."

"It's going to take a couple more days before I get used to these clothes myself," Eisenhower told them with a chuckle.

There was a parade for him. He stood in front of one of the hotels, with his arm across Mamie's shoulders, watching it go by and calling to old friends and neighbors. The high school band played, "I Like Ike." At the ball park, 20,000 people cheered him as he spoke.

After he and Mamie celebrated their 36th wedding anniversary in Denver, he dug in and began to fight for the nomination. He toured the country, giving speeches in little towns and big cities. He talked with farmers in their fields and with workers in factories. He made many whistle-stop talks from the rear platforms of trains.

The Republican National Convention was held in Chicago, during the first hot July days of 1952. Nominations were made on the fourth night.

Nomination of Senator Robert Taft, another Republican candidate, was made first. As his name was announced, there was a happy roar of voices. Taft's followers snatched banners and pennants and started parading up and down the aisles of the Amphitheater. Up and down and around they went, cheering Taft for forty-seven minutes.

Then Eisenhower was nominated. His supporters began shouting at the top of their voices. Some grabbed "We Want Ike" posters. Others held up placards with Ike's pic-

He made many whistle-stop talks

ture on them. And they all marched up and down and around, chanting, "We want Ike." The parade for Ike lasted for forty-six minutes.

Just before noon on the fifth day, the voting began. Several times Taft was in the lead. Then, when the last vote was cast, the ballots stood: Eisenhower 595, Taft 500. There was a great burst of cheering for Eisenhower.

Suddenly, over in the Minnesota section, Senator Edward J. Thye, who had voted for Taft, shouted, "Mr. Chairman, Minnesota wishes to change its vote to Eisenhower!"

Immediately there was a rush of other states to change their votes to Ike. Eisenhower won the nomination by a great majority. And the crowd in the Amphitheater went wild.

Ike had been watching the convention over television in his room in the Blackstone Hotel. With tear-filled eyes, he received the congratulations of his brothers, friends, and staff, who were with him. Then he went into the next room to see Mamie.

His next thought was for the defeated Taft. Ike pushed through the crowds and crossed the street to the Conrad Hilton Hotel.

There in the lobby, he and Taft shook hands before the excited crowd.

"I want to congratulate General Eisenhower," Taft said to them. "I shall do everything possible in the campaign to secure his election and to cooperate with him in his administration."

"I came to make a call of friendship on a very great American," Eisenhower responded. And he thanked Taft deeply for his willingness to work for the election.

Then Ike added, chuckling, that he had had a nightmare. "I dreamed I won both the nomination *and* the election," he said.

"You'll win, all right," Taft told him confidently.

Election day, November 4, Ike and Mamie spent at home in New York City with relatives. Ike's brothers, Arthur, Edgar, Earl, and Milton, came with their wives. Then there were Mamie's mother, and his son John's wife and their children. John, a major in the Army now, was in Korea where war again had flared up.

After dinner with the family, Ike, his brothers, and a few friends went to a suite in the Commodore Hotel to wait for the election returns.

There, with the telephone ringing and the teletype chattering, they watched and listened to the news which was being broadcast over television.

As the count of the ballots began to trickle in from various sections of the country, Eisenhower began to take the lead. He held the lead until he was so far ahead of Adlai Stevenson, the candidate of the Democratic Party, it was impossible for his opponent to catch up.

Along about ten o'clock, Eisenhower went down to the ballroom of the hotel to thank the 2,000 party workers for all they had done to help him.

They cheered him and shouted, "We like Ike! We like Ike!"

An hour later, he talked to the Citizens Committee for Eisenhower, and told them how grateful he was for all the work they had done.

A little before two o'clock the next morning, Adlai Stevenson conceded the election to Eisenhower. And he promised his support to the new President of the United States.

Eisenhower had polled well over thirty-three million votes, the largest vote ever received by a candidate for the Presidency. He had won in a landslide.

"Now you can rest," Mamie said, brushing the joyful tears from her eyes.

"That's what *you* think," he told her fondly. "The real job is just beginning."

About the Author

ARTHUR J. BECKHARD is a native New Yorker but has traveled from coast to coast many times and, as he says, has made all stops in between. He went to Ethical Culture High School, Amherst College, and the Columbia School of Journalism. Besides producing and directing fourteen plays on Broadway, Mr. Beckhard has written children's TV shows and several pictures for children, including two films starring Shirley Temple. His hobbies, when he has time for them, are photography and collecting early American glass.

About the Artist

CHARLES GEER was born in Long Island but now lives in New Jersey. He attended Dartmouth College and then went on to Pratt Institute to study art. From 1942 to 1945 he was on a navy destroyer in both the Atlantic and Pacific theaters of war. After the war ended he soon established himself as an artist. He has done both magazine and advertising art but is best known as a book illustrator, having illustrated many children's books for various publishers. In between assignments he does some sailing and camping, and once found time for a trip through Europe and the Middle East.

"Names That Made History"

ENID LAMONTE MEADOWCROFT, *Supervising Editor*

Born in Dennison, Texas,
October 14, 1890

2 Graduates from U.S. Military Academy
at West Point, 1915

3 Marries Mamie Doud on July 1, 1916

4 Takes command of first Armored
Tank School, March, 1918

9 Goes to Europe as Supreme Allied
Commander of the North Atlantic
Treaty Organization, 1950

10 Elected President of
the United States, 1952